ISBN 0-8373-4061-6

C-4061   CAREER EXAMINATION SERIES

This is your
PASSBOOK® for...

Elevator Apprentice

Test Preparation Study Guide

Questions & Answers

NATIONAL LEARNING CORPORATION

COPYRIGHT NOTICE

Copyright © 2019 by

National Learning Corporation

212 Michael Drive, Syosset, NY 11791
(516) 921-8888 • www.passbooks.com
E-mail: info@passbooks.com

PUBLISHED IN THE UNITED STATES OF AMERICA

PASSBOOK® SERIES

THE *PASSBOOK® SERIES* has been created to prepare applicants and candidates for the ultimate academic battlefield – the examination room.

At some time in our lives, each and every one of us may be required to take an examination – for validation, matriculation, admission, qualification, registration, certification, or licensure.

Based on the assumption that every applicant or candidate has met the basic formal educational standards, has taken the required number of courses, and read the necessary texts, the *PASSBOOK® SERIES* furnishes the one special preparation which may assure passing with confidence, instead of failing with insecurity. Examination questions – together with answers – are furnished as the basic vehicle for study so that the mysteries of the examination and its compounding difficulties may be eliminated or diminished by a sure method.

This book is meant to help you pass your examination provided that you qualify and are serious in your objective.

The entire field is reviewed through the huge store of content information which is succinctly presented through a provocative and challenging approach – the question-and-answer method.

A climate of success is established by furnishing the correct answers at the end of each test.

You soon learn to recognize types of questions, forms of questions, and patterns of questioning. You may even begin to anticipate expected outcomes.

You perceive that many questions are repeated or adapted so that you can gain acute insights, which may enable you to score many sure points.

You learn how to confront new questions, or types of questions, and to attack them confidently and work out the correct answers.

You note objectives and emphases, and recognize pitfalls and dangers, so that you may make positive educational adjustments.

Moreover, you are kept fully informed in relation to new concepts, methods, practices, and directions in the field.

You discover that you are actually taking the examination all the time: you are preparing for the examination by "taking" an examination, not by reading extraneous and/or supererogatory textbooks.

In short, this PASSBOOK®, used directedly, should be an important factor in helping you to pass your test.

ELEVATOR APPRENTICE

DUTIES
The Elevator Apprentice undergoes a period of training and instruction in the maintenance and repair of elevators. Works alongside skilled mechanics and assists while learning the trade.

SCOPE OF THE EXAMINATION
The written test will cover knowledge, skills and/or abilities in such areas as:

1. Mechanical aptitude;
2. Reading comprehension; and
3. Mathematical computation/Applied mathematics.

ELEVATOR APPRENTICE

JOB PURPOSE:
Responsible for assisting in the installation, maintenance and repair of the passenger and freight elevators, escalators, dumbwaiters and moving sidewalks under the direction of the Mechanic.

ESSENTIAL JOB FUNCTIONS:
Load unloads and moves materials, equipment and tools from vehicles to work areas; cleans elevator car tops, machine rooms, pits, rails and hoist ways within non-controlled climate field setting; paints machine rooms and pit; uses knowledge of elevator systems to assist mechanic in electrical and mechanical installation, repair or service operations; maintains elevator lighting fixtures; monitors equipment operation to determine faulty functioning. Performs related duties.

KNOWLEDGE
1. The ability to understand general arithmetic.
2. The ability to speak and write in a clear and understandable manner.
3. The ability to understand and follow verbal or written instructions.
4. The ability to learn, practice, and adhere to safety standards.

Mental Effort
1. The ability to maintain normal attention spans, with intermittent periods of high concentration, to assist the mechanic in electrical and mechanical installation, repair or service operations.
2. The ability to perform administrative duties such as data gathering and submitting written reports.

Physical
1. The ability to walk or stand.
2. The ability to lift up to 100 lbs.
3. The ability to perform repetitive stooping, forward bending and crouching.
4. The ability and willingness to travel.

Environmental
1. The ability to perform essential job functions in field setting with exposure to non-controlled climate conditions.
2. The ability and willingness to withstand heights and work in cramped working conditions.

Manual Dexterity
1. The ability to use hands, arms and feet for repetitive lifting.
2. The ability to use hands and arms to operate various hand and power tools and to record written information

Audible/Visual
1. The ability to communicate verbally.
2. The ability to observe essential functions for satisfactory job performance.
3. The ability to perceive color to distinguish color coded wiring components.

BASIC SKILLS TESTING

This validated basic skills exam is designed to measure your potential success in the elevator trade. Your abilities will be assessed in the areas of reading, mechanical comprehension, and arithmetic computation. The test is scored on a pass /fail basis, with 70% correct being the minimum passing grade.

Applicants who fail the test will NOT be interviewed and will be removed from the pool of applicants; however, they may re-apply during the next or subsequent recruitment period.

INTERVIEWING

Applicants who pass the test become eligible for the next step in the hiring process; the interview. Consistent with the projected employment needs, a hiring committee comprised of at least one individual from both the employer and the union will conduct interviews.
A sufficient amount of time will be allotted to each interview session to allow for adequate consideration of the following grading areas:
- Work experience
- School record
- Mechanical abilities
- Motivation

After a brief introduction, the committee will ask questions of the applicant with the purpose of learning as much about the applicant as possible and about the applicant's capacity to participate in apprenticeship. Responses to interview questions will be written down at the time of the interview to provide a record for the applicant's file. All applicants will be asked the same questions, and the hiring committee will assess each applicant on a scale of 100. Applicants scoring 69 points and below on the interview assessment will not be considered for apprenticeship.

SELECTING APPRENTICES

Those individuals with a composite score of 70 or higher on the interview assessment will be placed on a ranked list, with the highest scoring individuals placed at the top of the list. The Apprenticeship Committee will notify all applicants of the results of the interview, including their score and ranking. Applicants will be placed as apprentices based on their rank in this pool of eligible candidates.

Applicants not selected shall remain on the ranked list for a period of two years. Final approval or rejection of an application will be made by the JAC, which will review the applicant's eligibility for entry into the Program and the availability of apprentices and mechanics in the applicant's geographic area. If the application is rejected, the applicant will be notified of the rejection and the reason therefore.

HOW TO TAKE A TEST

You have studied long, hard and conscientiously.

With your official admission card in hand, and your heart pounding, you have been admitted to the examination room.

You note that there are several hundred other applicants in the examination room waiting to take the same test.

They all appear to be equally well prepared.

You know that nothing but your best effort will suffice. The "moment of truth" is at hand: you now have to demonstrate objectively, in writing, your knowledge of content and your understanding of subject matter.

You are fighting the most important battle of your life—to pass and/or score high on an examination which will determine your career and provide the economic basis for your livelihood.

What extra, special things should you know and should you do in taking the examination?

I. YOU MUST PASS AN EXAMINATION

A. WHAT EVERY CANDIDATE SHOULD KNOW

Examination applicants often ask us for help in preparing for the written test. What can I study in advance? What kinds of questions will be asked? How will the test be given? How will the papers be graded?

B. HOW ARE EXAMS DEVELOPED?

Examinations are carefully written by trained technicians who are specialists in the field known as "psychological measurement," in consultation with recognized authorities in the field of work that the test will cover. These experts recommend the subject matter areas or skills to be tested; only those knowledges or skills important to your success on the job are included. The most reliable books and source materials available are used as references. Together, the experts and technicians judge the difficulty level of the questions.

Test technicians know how to phrase questions so that the problem is clearly stated. Their ethics do not permit "trick" or "catch" questions. Questions may have been tried out on sample groups, or subjected to statistical analysis, to determine their usefulness.

Written tests are often used in combination with performance tests, ratings of training and experience, and oral interviews. All of these measures combine to form the best-known means of finding the right person for the right job.

II. HOW TO PASS THE WRITTEN TEST

A. BASIC STEPS

1) Study the announcement

How, then, can you know what subjects to study? Our best answer is: "Learn as much as possible about the class of positions for which you've applied." The exam will test the knowledge, skills and abilities needed to do the work.

Your most valuable source of information about the position you want is the official exam announcement. This announcement lists the training and experience qualifications. Check these standards and apply only if you come reasonably close to meeting them. Many jurisdictions preview the written test in the exam announcement by including a section called "Knowledge and Abilities Required," "Scope of the Examination," or some similar heading. Here you will find out specifically what fields will be tested.

2) Choose appropriate study materials

If the position for which you are applying is technical or advanced, you will read more advanced, specialized material. If you are already familiar with the basic principles of your field, elementary textbooks would waste your time. Concentrate on advanced textbooks and technical periodicals. Think through the concepts and review difficult problems in your field.

These are all general sources. You can get more ideas on your own initiative, following these leads. For example, training manuals and publications of the government agency which employs workers in your field can be useful, particularly for technical and professional positions. A letter or visit to the government department involved may result in more specific study suggestions, and certainly will provide you with a more definite idea of the exact nature of the position you are seeking.

3) Study this book!

III. KINDS OF TESTS

Tests are used for purposes other than measuring knowledge and ability to perform specified duties. For some positions, it is equally important to test ability to make adjustments to new situations or to profit from training. In others, basic mental abilities not dependent on information are essential. Questions which test these things may not appear as pertinent to the duties of the position as those which test for knowledge and information. Yet they are often highly important parts of a fair examination. For very general questions, it is almost impossible to help you direct your study efforts. What we can do is to point out some of the more common of these general abilities needed in public service positions and describe some typical questions.

1) General information

Broad, general information has been found useful for predicting job success in some kinds of work. This is tested in a variety of ways, from vocabulary lists to questions about current events. Basic background in some field of work, such as sociology or economics, may be sampled in a group of questions. Often these are principles which have become familiar to most persons through exposure rather than through formal training. It is difficult to advise you how to study for these questions; being alert to the world around you is our best suggestion.

2) Verbal ability

An example of an ability needed in many positions is verbal or language ability. Verbal ability is, in brief, the ability to use and understand words. Vocabulary and grammar tests are typical measures of this ability. Reading comprehension or paragraph interpretation questions are common in many kinds of civil service tests. You are given a paragraph of written material and asked to find its central meaning.

IV. KINDS OF QUESTIONS

1. Multiple-choice Questions

Most popular of the short-answer questions is the "multiple choice" or "best answer" question. It can be used, for example, to test for factual knowledge, ability to solve problems or judgment in meeting situations found at work.

A multiple-choice question is normally one of three types:

- It can begin with an incomplete statement followed by several possible endings. You are to find the one ending which *best* completes the statement, although some of the others may not be entirely wrong.
- It can also be a complete statement in the form of a question which is answered by choosing one of the statements listed.
- It can be in the form of a problem – again you select the best answer.

Here is an example of a multiple-choice question with a discussion which should give you some clues as to the method for choosing the right answer:

When an employee has a complaint about his assignment, the action which will *best* help him overcome his difficulty is to
- A. discuss his difficulty with his coworkers
- B. take the problem to the head of the organization
- C. take the problem to the person who gave him the assignment
- D. say nothing to anyone about his complaint

In answering this question, you should study each of the choices to find which is best. Consider choice "A" – Certainly an employee may discuss his complaint with fellow employees, but no change or improvement can result, and the complaint remains unresolved. Choice "B" is a poor choice since the head of the organization probably does not know what assignment you have been given, and taking your problem to him is known as "going over the head" of the supervisor. The supervisor, or person who made the assignment, is the person who can clarify it or correct any injustice. Choice "C" is, therefore, correct. To say nothing, as in choice "D," is unwise. Supervisors have and interest in knowing the problems employees are facing, and the employee is seeking a solution to his problem.

2. True/False

3. Matching Questions

Matching an answer from a column of choices within another column.

V. RECORDING YOUR ANSWERS

Computer terminals are used more and more today for many different kinds of exams. For an examination with very few applicants, you may be told to record your answers in the test booklet itself. Separate answer sheets are much more common. If this separate answer sheet is to be scored by machine – and this is often the case – it is highly important that you mark your answers correctly in order to get credit.

VI. BEFORE THE TEST

YOUR PHYSICAL CONDITION IS IMPORTANT

If you are not well, you can't do your best work on tests. If you are half asleep, you can't do your best either. Here are some tips:

1) Get about the same amount of sleep you usually get. Don't stay up all night before the test, either partying or worrying—DON'T DO IT!
2) If you wear glasses, be sure to wear them when you go to take the test. This goes for hearing aids, too.
3) If you have any physical problems that may keep you from doing your best, be sure to tell the person giving the test. If you are sick or in poor health, you relay cannot do your best on any test. You can always come back and take the test some other time.

Common sense will help you find procedures to follow to get ready for an examination. Too many of us, however, overlook these sensible measures. Indeed, nervousness and fatigue have been found to be the most serious reasons why applicants fail to do their best on civil service tests. Here is a list of reminders:

- Begin your preparation early – Don't wait until the last minute to go scurrying around for books and materials or to find out what the position is all about.
- Prepare continuously – An hour a night for a week is better than an all-night cram session. This has been definitely established. What is more, a night a week for a month will return better dividends than crowding your study into a shorter period of time.
- Locate the place of the exam – You have been sent a notice telling you when and where to report for the examination. If the location is in a different town or otherwise unfamiliar to you, it would be well to inquire the best route and learn something about the building.
- Relax the night before the test – Allow your mind to rest. Do not study at all that night. Plan some mild recreation or diversion; then go to bed early and get a good night's sleep.
- Get up early enough to make a leisurely trip to the place for the test – This way unforeseen events, traffic snarls, unfamiliar buildings, etc. will not upset you.
- Dress comfortably – A written test is not a fashion show. You will be known by number and not by name, so wear something comfortable.
- Leave excess paraphernalia at home – Shopping bags and odd bundles will get in your way. You need bring only the items mentioned in the official notice you received; usually everything you need is provided. Do not bring reference books to the exam. They will only confuse these last minutes and be taken away from you when in the test room.

- Arrive somewhat ahead of time – If because of transportation schedules you must get there very early, bring a newspaper or magazine to take your mind off yourself while waiting.
- Locate the examination room – When you have found the proper room, you will be directed to the seat or part of the room where you will sit. Sometimes you are given a sheet of instructions to read while you are waiting. Do not fill out any forms until you are told to do so; just read them and be prepared.
- Relax and prepare to listen to the instructions
- If you have any physical problem that may keep you from doing your best, be sure to tell the test administrator. If you are sick or in poor health, you really cannot do your best on the exam. You can come back and take the test some other time.

VII. AT THE TEST

The day of the test is here and you have the test booklet in your hand. The temptation to get going is very strong. Caution! There is more to success than knowing the right answers. You must know how to identify your papers and understand variations in the type of short-answer question used in this particular examination. Follow these suggestions for maximum results from your efforts:

1) Cooperate with the monitor
The test administrator has a duty to create a situation in which you can be as much at ease as possible. He will give instructions, tell you when to begin, check to see that you are marking your answer sheet correctly, and so on. He is not there to guard you, although he will see that your competitors do not take unfair advantage. He wants to help you do your best.

2) Listen to all instructions
Don't jump the gun! Wait until you understand all directions. In most civil service tests you get more time than you need to answer the questions. So don't be in a hurry. Read each word of instructions until you clearly understand the meaning. Study the examples, listen to all announcements and follow directions. Ask questions if you do not understand what to do.

3) Identify your papers
Civil service exams are usually identified by number only. You will be assigned a number; you must not put your name on your test papers. Be sure to copy your number correctly. Since more than one exam may be given, copy your exact examination title.

4) Plan your time
Unless you are told that a test is a "speed" or "rate of work" test, speed itself is usually not important. Time enough to answer all the questions will be provided, but this does not mean that you have all day. An overall time limit has been set. Divide the total time (in minutes) by the number of questions to determine the approximate time you have for each question.

5) Do not linger over difficult questions
If you come across a difficult question, mark it with a paper clip (useful to have along) and come back to it when you have been through the booklet. One caution if you do this – be sure to skip a number on your answer sheet as well. Check often to be sure that you

have not lost your place and that you are marking in the row numbered the same as the question you are answering.

6) Read the questions

Be sure you know what the question asks! Many capable people are unsuccessful because they failed to *read* the questions correctly.

7) Answer all questions

Unless you have been instructed that a penalty will be deducted for incorrect answers, it is better to guess than to omit a question.

8) Speed tests

It is often better NOT to guess on speed tests. It has been found that on timed tests people are tempted to spend the last few seconds before time is called in marking answers at random – without even reading them – in the hope of picking up a few extra points. To discourage this practice, the instructions may warn you that your score will be "corrected" for guessing. That is, a penalty will be applied. The incorrect answers will be deducted from the correct ones, or some other penalty formula will be used.

9) Review your answers

If you finish before time is called, go back to the questions you guessed or omitted to give them further thought. Review other answers if you have time.

10) Return your test materials

If you are ready to leave before others have finished or time is called, take ALL your materials to the monitor and leave quietly. Never take any test material with you. The monitor can discover whose papers are not complete, and taking a test booklet may be grounds for disqualification.

VIII. EXAMINATION TECHNIQUES

1) Read the general instructions carefully. These are usually printed on the first page of the exam booklet. As a rule, these instructions refer to the timing of the examination; the fact that you should not start work until the signal and must stop work at a signal, etc. If there are any *special* instructions, such as a choice of questions to be answered, make sure that you note this instruction carefully.

2) When you are ready to start work on the examination, that is as soon as the signal has been given, read the instructions to each question booklet, underline any key words or phrases, such as *least, best, outline, describe* and the like. In this way you will tend to answer as requested rather than discover on reviewing your paper that you *listed without describing*, that you selected the *worst* choice rather than the *best* choice, etc.

3) If the examination is of the objective or multiple-choice type – that is, each question will also give a series of possible answers: A, B, C or D, and you are called upon to select the best answer and write the letter next to that answer on your answer paper – it is advisable to start answering each question in turn. There may be anywhere from 50 to 100 such questions in the three or four hours allotted and you can see how much time would be taken if you read through all the questions before beginning to answer any. Furthermore, if you come across a

question or group of questions which you know would be difficult to answer, it would undoubtedly affect your handling of all the other questions.

4) If the examination is of the essay type and contains but a few questions, it is a moot point as to whether you should read all the questions before starting to answer any one. Of course, if you are given a choice – say five out of seven and the like – then it is essential to read all the questions so you can eliminate the two that are most difficult. If, however, you are asked to answer all the questions, there may be danger in trying to answer the easiest one first because you may find that you will spend too much time on it. The best technique is to answer the first question, then proceed to the second, etc.

5) Time your answers. Before the exam begins, write down the time it started, then add the time allowed for the examination and write down the time it must be completed, then divide the time available somewhat as follows:
   - If 3-1/2 hours are allowed, that would be 210 minutes. If you have 80 objective-type questions, that would be an average of 2-1/2 minutes per question. Allow yourself no more than 2 minutes per question, or a total of 160 minutes, which will permit about 50 minutes to review.
   - If for the time allotment of 210 minutes there are 7 essay questions to answer, that would average about 30 minutes a question. Give yourself only 25 minutes per question so that you have about 35 minutes to review.

6) The most important instruction is to *read each question* and make sure you know what is wanted. The second most important instruction is to *time yourself properly* so that you answer every question. The third most important instruction is to *answer every question*. Guess if you have to but include something for each question. Remember that you will receive no credit for a blank and will probably receive some credit if you write something in answer to an essay question. If you guess a letter – say "B" for a multiple-choice question – you may have guessed right. If you leave a blank as an answer to a multiple-choice question, the examiners may respect your feelings but it will not add a point to your score. Some exams may penalize you for wrong answers, so in such cases *only*, you may not want to guess unless you have some basis for your answer.

7) Suggestions
   a. Objective-type questions
      1. Examine the question booklet for proper sequence of pages and questions
      2. Read all instructions carefully
      3. Skip any question which seems too difficult; return to it after all other questions have been answered
      4. Apportion your time properly; do not spend too much time on any single question or group of questions
      5. Note and underline key words – *all, most, fewest, least, best, worst, same, opposite,* etc.
      6. Pay particular attention to negatives
      7. Note unusual option, e.g., unduly long, short, complex, different or similar in content to the body of the question
      8. Observe the use of "hedging" words – *probably, may, most likely,* etc.
      9. Make sure that your answer is put next to the same number as the question

10. Do not second-guess unless you have good reason to believe the second answer is definitely more correct
11. Cross out original answer if you decide another answer is more accurate; do not erase until you are ready to hand your paper in
12. Answer all questions; guess unless instructed otherwise
13. Leave time for review

b. Essay questions
   1. Read each question carefully
   2. Determine exactly what is wanted. Underline key words or phrases.
   3. Decide on outline or paragraph answer
   4. Include many different points and elements unless asked to develop any one or two points or elements
   5. Show impartiality by giving pros and cons unless directed to select one side only
   6. Make and write down any assumptions you find necessary to answer the questions
   7. Watch your English, grammar, punctuation and choice of words
   8. Time your answers; don't crowd material

8) Answering the essay question

Most essay questions can be answered by framing the specific response around several key words or ideas. Here are a few such key words or ideas:

M's: manpower, materials, methods, money, management
P's: purpose, program, policy, plan, procedure, practice, problems, pitfalls, personnel, public relations

a. Six basic steps in handling problems:
   1. Preliminary plan and background development
   2. Collect information, data and facts
   3. Analyze and interpret information, data and facts
   4. Analyze and develop solutions as well as make recommendations
   5. Prepare report and sell recommendations
   6. Install recommendations and follow up effectiveness

b. Pitfalls to avoid
1. *Taking things for granted* – A statement of the situation does not necessarily imply that each of the elements is necessarily true; for example, a complaint may be invalid and biased so that all that can be taken for granted is that a complaint has been registered
2. *Considering only one side of a situation* – Wherever possible, indicate several alternatives and then point out the reasons you selected the best one
3. *Failing to indicate follow up* – Whenever your answer indicates action on your part, make certain that you will take proper follow-up action to see how successful your recommendations, procedures or actions turn out to be
4. *Taking too long in answering any single question* Remember to time your answers properly

———

EXAMINATION SECTION

MECHANICAL APTITUDE

EXAMINATION SECTION
TEST 1

MECHANICAL COMPREHENSION

DIRECTIONS: Questions 1 to 4 test your ability to understand general mechanical devices. Pictures are shown and questions asked about the mechanical devices shown in the picture. Read each question and study the picture. Each question is followed by four choices. For each question, choose the one BEST answer (A, B, C, or D). Then *PRINT THE LETTER OF THE CORRECT ANSWER IN THE SPACE AT THE RIGHT.*

1. The reason for crossing the belt connecting these wheels is to

1.____

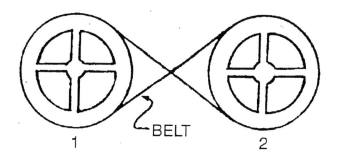

   A.   make the wheels turn in opposite directions
   B.   make wheel 2 turn faster than wheel 1
   C.   save wear on the belt
   D.   take up slack in the belt

2. The purpose of the small gear between the two large gears is to

2.____

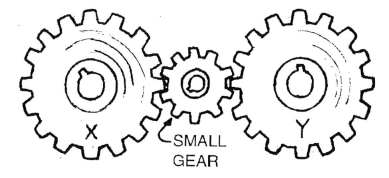

   A.   increase the speed of the larger gears
   B.   allow the larger gears to turn in different directions
   C.   decrease the speed of the larger gears
   D.   make the larger gears turn in the same direction

3. Each of these three-foot-high water cans have a bottom with an area of-one square foot.   3.____
The pressure on the bottom of the cans is

A   B   C

A. least in A   B. least in B
C. least in C   D. the same in all

4. The reading on the scale should be   4.____

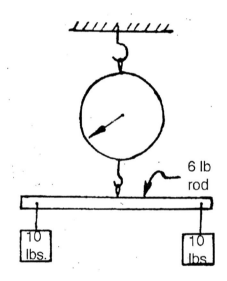

6 lb rod

A. zero
B. 10 pounds
C. 13 pounds
D. 26 pounds

KEY (CORRECT ANSWERS)

1. A
2. D
3. D
4. D

TEST 2

DIRECTIONS: Questions 1 to 6 test knowledge of tools and how to use them. For each question, decide which one of the four things shown in the boxes labeled A, B, C, or D normally is used with or goes best with the thing in the picture on the left. Then *PRINT THE LETTER OF THE CORRECT ANSWER IN THE SPACE AT THE RIGHT.*

NOTE: All tools are NOT drawn to the same scale.

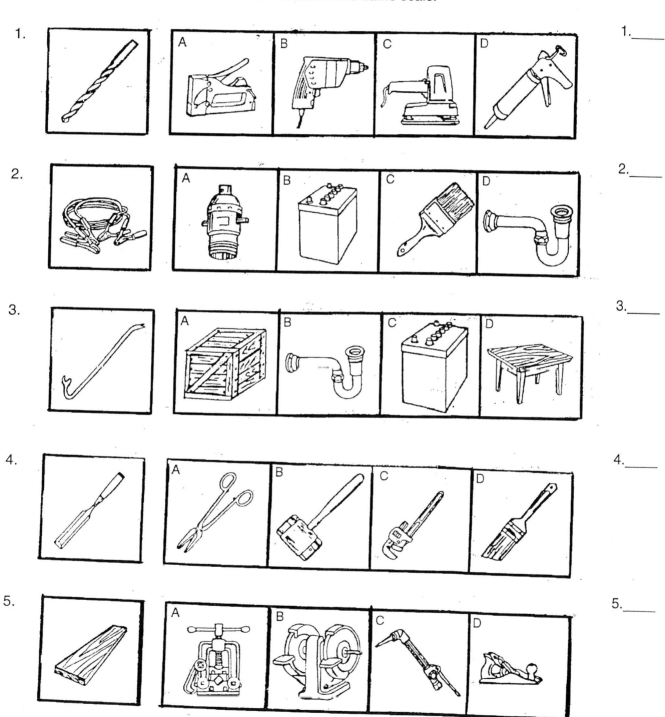

1.____

2.____

3.____

4.____

5.____

6.

KEY (CORRECT ANSWERS)

1.	B		4.	B
2.	B		5.	D
3.	A		6.	B

MECHANICAL APTITUDE

EXAMINATION SECTION
TEST 1

QUESTIONS 1-6.

Questions 1 through 6 are questions designed to test your ability to distinguish identical forms from unlike forms.

In each question, there are five drawings, lettered A, B, C, D, and E. Four of the drawings are alike. You are to find the one drawing that is different from the other four in the question. Then, on the Answer Sheet, blacken the space lettered the same as the figure that you have selected.

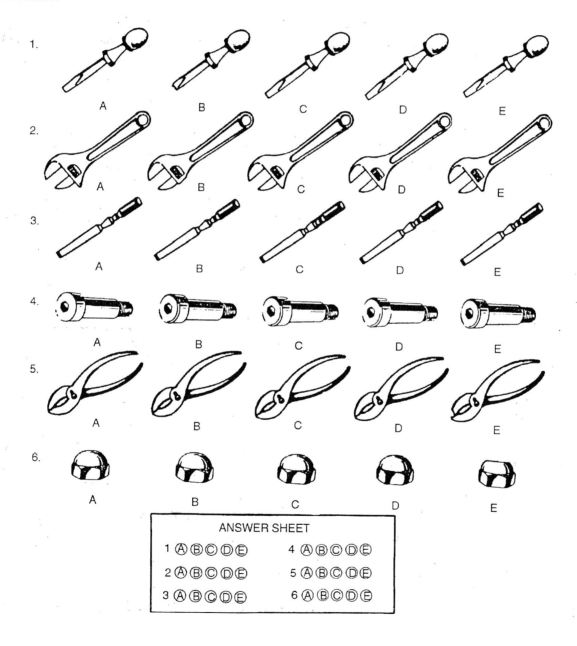

ANSWER SHEET

1 Ⓐ Ⓑ Ⓒ Ⓓ Ⓔ   4 Ⓐ Ⓑ Ⓒ Ⓓ Ⓔ

2 Ⓐ Ⓑ Ⓒ Ⓓ Ⓔ   5 Ⓐ Ⓑ Ⓒ Ⓓ Ⓔ

3 Ⓐ Ⓑ Ⓒ Ⓓ Ⓔ   6 Ⓐ Ⓑ Ⓒ Ⓓ Ⓔ

QUESTIONS 7-8.

Questions 7 and 8 are questions designed to test your knowledge of pattern matching.

Questions 7 and 8 present problems found in making patterns. Each shows, at the left side, two or more separate flat pieces. In each question, select the arrangement lettered A, B, C, or D that shows how these pieces at the left can be fitted together without gaps or overlapping. The pieces may be turned around or turned over in any way to make them fit together.

On the Answer Sheet blacken the space lettered the same as the figure that you have selected.

Now, look at the questions below.

7. From these pieces, which one of these arrangements can you make?

A   B   C   D

In question 7, only the arrangement D can be made from the pieces shown at the left, so space D is marked for Question 7 on the answer sheet below. (Note that it is necessary to turn the pieces around so that the short sides are at the bottom in the arrangement lettered D. None of the other arrangements show pieces of the given size and shape.)

8. From these pieces, which one of these arrangements can you make?

A   B   C   D

ANSWER SHEET

7 Ⓐ Ⓑ Ⓒ Ⓓ

8 Ⓐ Ⓑ Ⓒ Ⓓ

QUESTIONS 9-10.

Questions 9 and 10. are questions designed to test your ability to identify forms of *LIKE* and *UNLIKE* proportions.

In each of the questions, select from the drawings of objects labeled A, B, C, and D, the one that would have the Top, Front, and Right views shown in the drawing at the left. Then on your Answer Sheet blacken the space that has the same letter as your answer.

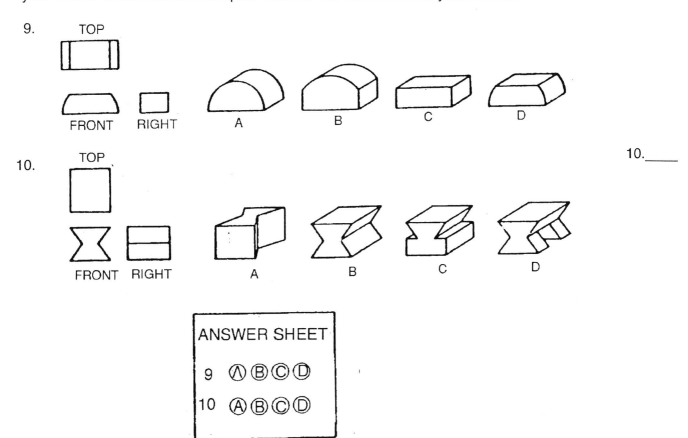

9. TOP

FRONT   RIGHT   A   B   C   D

10. TOP

FRONT   RIGHT   A   B   C   D

10.____

ANSWER SHEET

9 Ⓐ Ⓑ Ⓒ Ⓓ

10 Ⓐ Ⓑ Ⓒ Ⓓ

QUESTIONS 11-14.

Explanation and Commentary:
In each question, ONE rectangle is clearly WRONG. For each question, use the measuirng gage to check each of the rectangles and to find the WRONG one. Do this by putting the measuring gage rectangle on the question rectangle with the same letter so that the rectangles slightly overlap and the thin lines are parallel, like the one at the right. In this case, the height of the question rectangle exactly matches the height of the measuring gage rectangle, so the question rectangle is the right height. In this case, you do NOT mark your answer sheet.

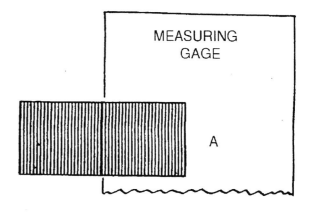

MEASURING GAGE

A

Once in every question, when you put a measuring gage rectangle on a question rectangle, you will find that the heights do *NOT* match and that the question rectangle is clearly wrong, like the one at the right. In this case, you mark on the answer sheet the space with the same letter as the wrong rectangle. *REMEMBER TO LINE UP THE MEASURING RECTANGLE WITH EACH QUESTION RECTANGLE SO THAT THE THIN LINES ARE EXACTLY PARALLEL.*

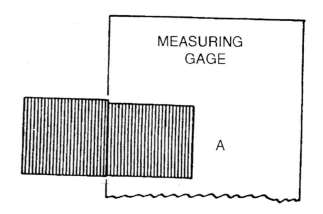

Now, cut out the measuring gage on the last page and practice on the questions. The test will be timed, so practice doing them rapidly and accurately.

Questions 11 through 14 test how quickly and accurately you can check the heights of rectangles with a measuring gage. Each question has five rectangles of different heights. The height is the dimension that runs the same way as the thin lines.

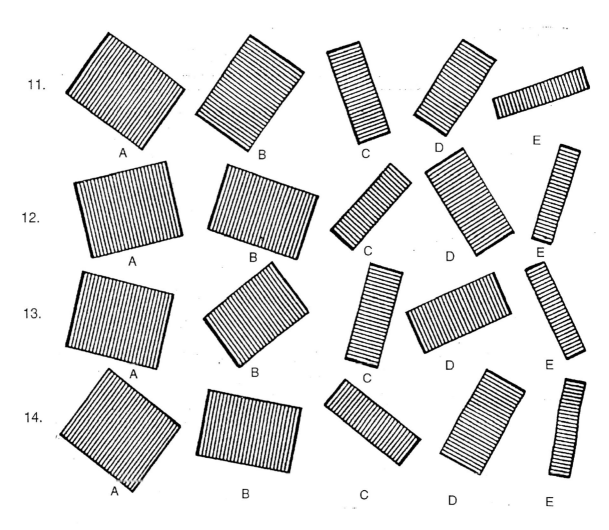

ANSWER SHEET

11 Ⓐ Ⓑ Ⓒ Ⓓ Ⓔ

12 Ⓐ Ⓑ Ⓒ Ⓓ Ⓔ

13 Ⓐ Ⓑ Ⓒ Ⓓ Ⓔ

14 Ⓐ Ⓑ Ⓒ Ⓓ Ⓔ

MEASURING
GAGE

 A

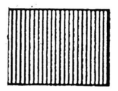 B

 C

 D

 E

KEY (CORRECT ANSWERS)

1.	B	8.	B
2.	B	9.	D
3.	C	10.	B
4.	A	11.	D
5.	E	12.	C
6.	E	13.	B
7.	D	14.	A

EXAMINATION SECTION
TEST 1

DIRECTIONS: Each question or incomplete statement is followed by two suggested answers or completions. Select A or B, or C if the two figures have the same value, as the BEST answer that completes the statement or completes the statement. *PRINT THE LETTER OF THE CORRECT ANSWER IN THE SPACE AT THE RIGHT.*

1.

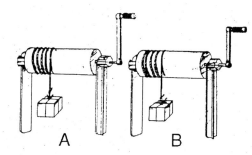

With which windlass can a man raise the heavier weight?

1.____

2.

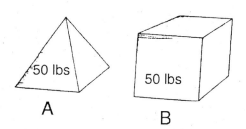

Which of these solid blocks will be the harder to tip over?

2.____

3.

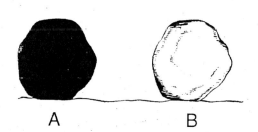

Which rock will get hotter in the sun?

3.____

4.

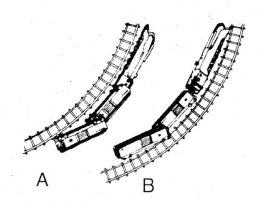

Which of these is the more likely picture of a train wreck?

4.____

5.

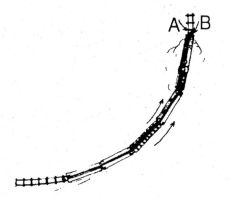

If the track is exactly level, on which rail does more pressure come?

5.____

6.

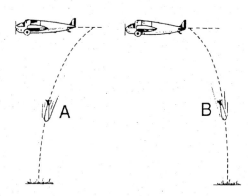

Which picture shows the way a bomb falls from a moving airplane if there is no wind?

6.____

7.

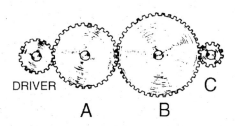

Indicate a gear which turn the same direction as the driver.

7.____

8.

If there are no clouds, on which night will you be able to see more stars?

8.____

9.

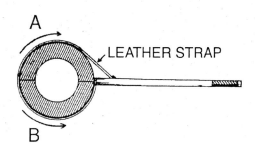

This wrench can be used to turn the pipe in direction:

9.____

10.

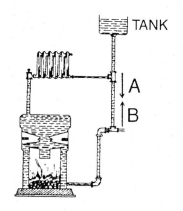

In which direction does the water in the right-hand pipe go?

10.____

11.

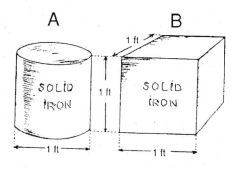

Which weighs more?

11.____

12.

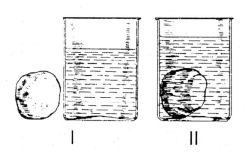

If the rock and tank of water together in picture I weigh 100 pounds, what will they weigh in picture II?

12.____

13.

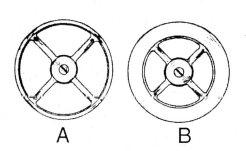

Which steel wheel will keep going longer after the power has been shut off?

13.____

14.

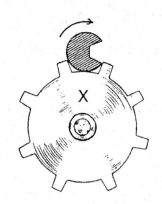

The top of the wheel X will go
- A. steadily to the right
- B. steadily to the left
- C. by jerks to the left

14.____

15.

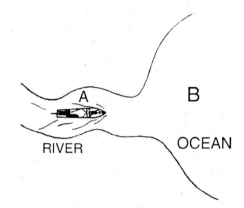

At which point will the boat be lower in the water?

15.____

16.

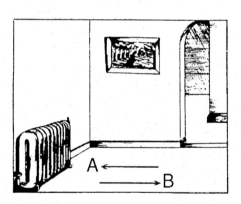

Which arrow shows the way the air will move along the floor when the radiator is turned on?

16.____

17.

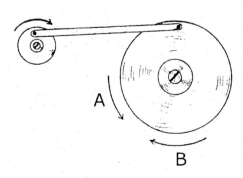

When the little wheel turns around, the big wheel will
- A. turn in direction A
- B. turn in direction B
- C. move back and forth

17.____

18.

A   B

Which boy gets more light on the pages of his book?

18.____

19.

Which weighs more?

19.____

20.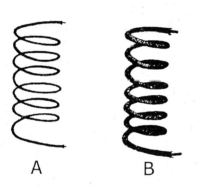

A   B

Which of these wires offers more resistance to the passage of an electric current?

20.____

21.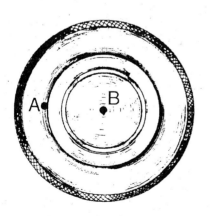

Which spot on the wheel travels faster?

21.____

22.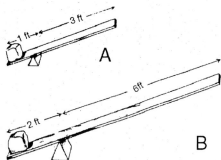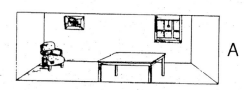

With which arrangement can a man lift the heavier weight?

22.____

23.

Which room has more of an echo?

23.____

24.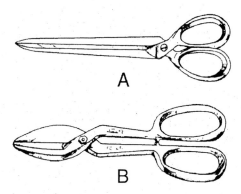

Which would be the BETTER shears for cutting metal?

24.____

KEY (CORRECT ANSWERS)

1. A	11. B
2. A	12. C
3. A	13. B
4. A	14. C
5. B	15. A
6. A	16. A
7. B	17. C
8. B	18. A
9. A	19. A
10. A	20. A

21. B
22. B
23. A
24. B

———

MECHANICAL APTITUDE

MECHANICAL REASONING
DIRECTIONS

This test consists of a number of pictures and questions about those pictures. Look at Example X on this page to see just what to do. Example X shows a picture of two men carrying a machine part on a board and asks, "Which man has the heavier load? If equal, mark C." Man "B" has the heavier load because the weight is closer to him than to man "A," so on the separate Answer Sheet you would fill in the space under B, like this

Now look at Example Y. The question asks, "Which weighs more? If equal, mark C." As the scale is perfectly balanced, "A" and "B" must weigh the same, so you would blacken the space

under C on your separate Answer Sheet, like this

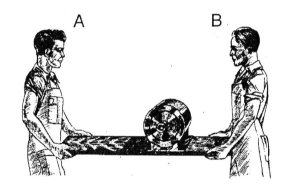

X

Which man has the heavier load?
(If equal, mark C.)

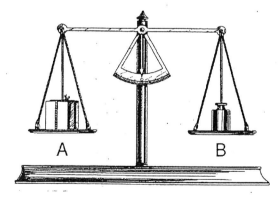

Y

Which weighs more?
(If equal, mark C.)

On the following pages there are more pictures and questions. Read each question carefully, look at the picture, and mark your answer on the separate Answer Sheet. Do not forget that there is a third choice for every question.

1

When these soldiers march around
the corner, which man goes further?
(If equal, mark C.)

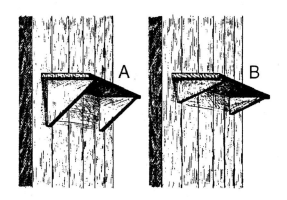

2

Which shelf is stronger?
(If equal, mark C.)

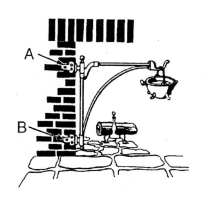

3

Which hinge is more likely to pull out
of the brick wall?
(If equal, mark C.)

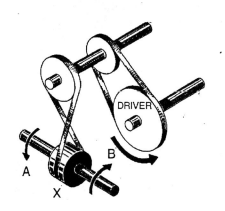

4

If the driver turns in the direction
shown, which way will the pulley at "X"
turn?
(If either, mark C.)

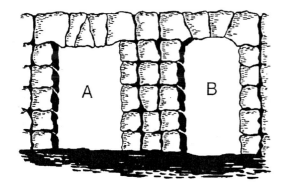

5

Which archway is stronger?
(If equal, mark C.)

6

In which picture can the ferry cross
the river more quickly?
(If either, mark C.)

7

When the bottom pulley turns in the
direction shown, which way does the
top pulley turn?
(If either, mark C.)

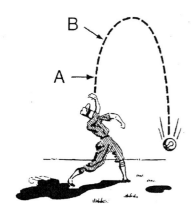

8

At which point was the ball going
faster?
(If equal, mark C.)

9

When the left-hand gear turns in the direction shown, which way does the right-hand one turn?
(If either, mark C.)

10

Which tread must stop for the tank to turn in the direction shown?
(If neither, mark C.)

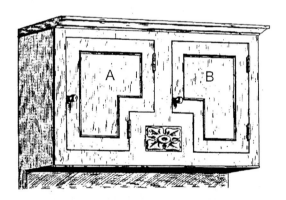

11

Which door will swing better on its hinges?
(If neither, mark C.)

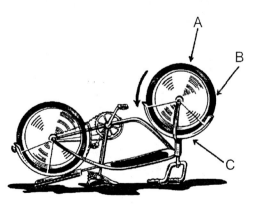

12

When the bicycle wheel stops moving, which arrow shows where the tire valve will stop?

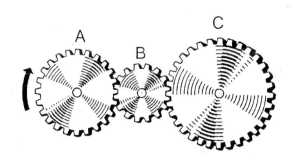

13

Which gear turns the least number of times in a minute?

14

Which picture shows the easier way for the men to lift the pipe?
(If equal, mark C.)

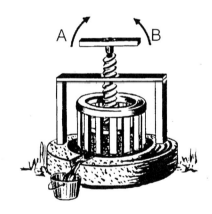

15

Which way should the handle be turned to press juice from fruit?
(If either, mark C.)

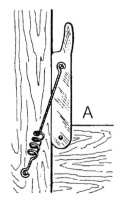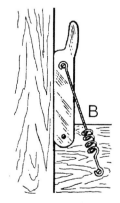

16

In which picture will the spring hold the handle where it now is?
(If both, mark C.)

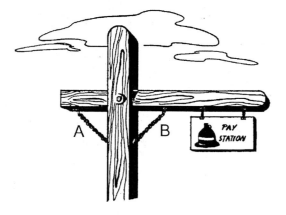

17

Which chain alone will hold up the sign?
(If either, mark C.)

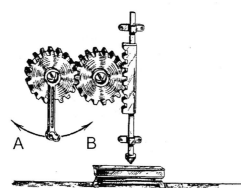

18

Which way should the handle be moved to push the point against the plate?
(If either, mark C.)

19

Which girl can lift the bucket of water more easily?
(If equal, mark C.)

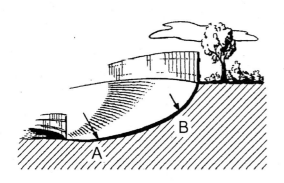

20

On which part of this race track will a very fast car make the turn?
(If either, mark C.)

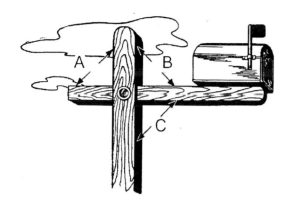

21

Which letter shows the best place for a chain support?

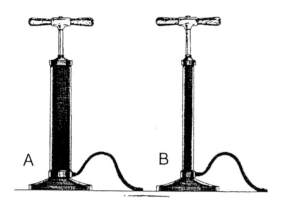

22

With which pump can you blow up a tube for swimming more quickly?
(If either, mark C.)

23

Which wheel will turn more slowly?
(If equal, mark C.)

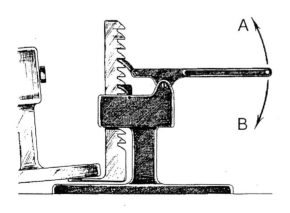

24

This jack lifts when the handle is moved in:
    (A)   direction A;
    (B)   direction B;
    (C)   either direction.

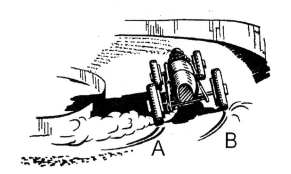

25

In racing around this track, which wheel travels further?
(If equal, mark C.)

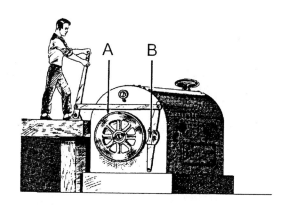

26

Which part will wear out more quickly if both the brake and wheel are made of iron?
(If equal, mark C.)

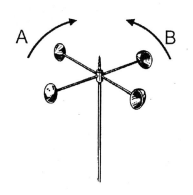

27

When the wind blows, in which direction will these cups turn?
(If either, mark C.)

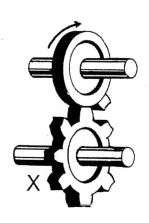

28

When the upper wheel turns in the direction shown, the top of the lower wheel will move:
  (A) steadily to the left;
  (B) by jerks to the right;
  (C) by jerks to the left.

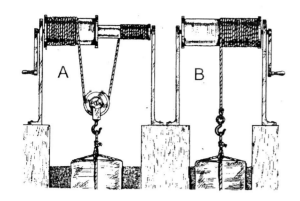

29

With which windlass can the heavier weight be lifted?
(If equal, mark C.)

30

Which picture shows the path of a thrown ball?
(If either, mark C.)

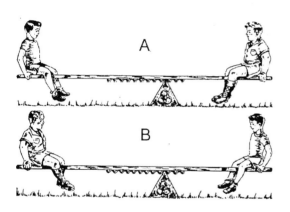

31

Which picture shows how the two boys will balance better?
(If equal, markC.)

32

In which direction must the propeller turn to drive the ship forward?
(If either, mark C.)

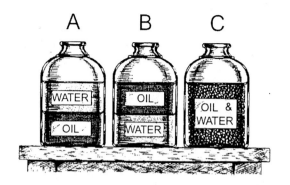

33

Which picture shows how oil and water would be after standing for a while?

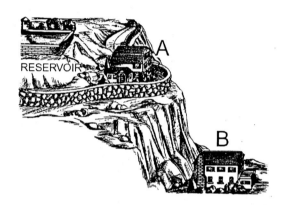

34

At which house will a hose throw water further?
(If either, mark C.)

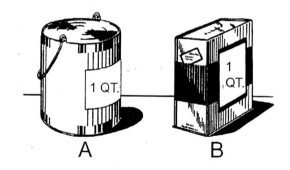

35

Which shape can will need the bigger carton for a dozen quarts?
(If equal, mark C.)

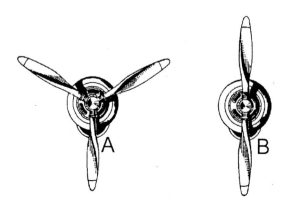

36

Which propeller needs the more powerful engine to turn it at a given speed?
(If equal, mark C.)

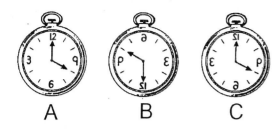

37

Which picture shows how a clock looks when seen in a mirror?

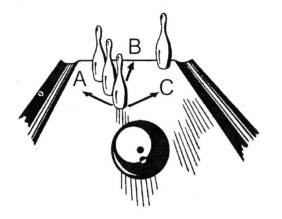

38

Which way will the pin go after the bowling ball hits it?

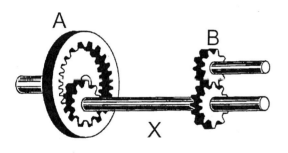

39

Which gear turns the same way as shaft "X"?
(If both, mark C.)

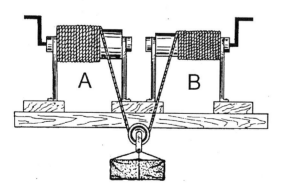

40

Which windlass must be turned more times to lift the weight five feet?
(If equal, mark C.)

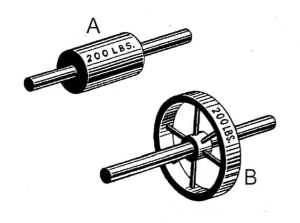

41

Which flywheel will keep its shaft turning longer?
(If equal, mark C.)

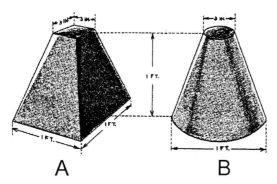

42

Which weighs less?
(If equal, mark C.)

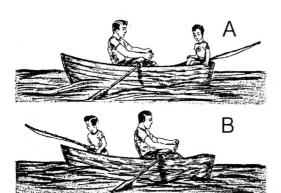

43

Which boat will be easier to row?
(If equal, mark C.)

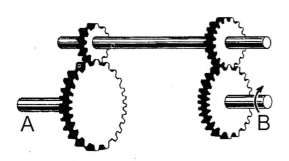

44

Which shaft will turn faster?
(If equal, mark C.)

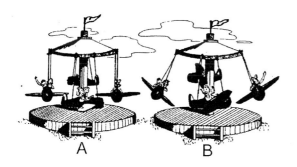

45

In which picture are the children pressed more firmly against the seats?
(If equal, markC.)

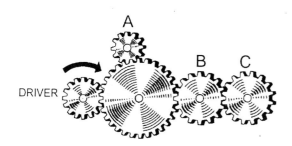

46

Which gear turns opposite to the driver?

47

Which will carry more water, the two pipes in A or the one pipe in B?
(If equal, mark C.)

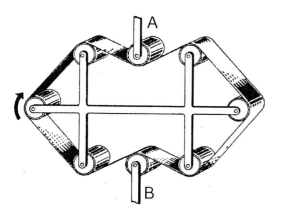

48

Which roller turns in the direction opposite to "X"?
(If both, mark C.)

49

In which loop is the pilot more likely to
fall out of the plane?
(If equal, mark C.)

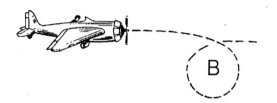

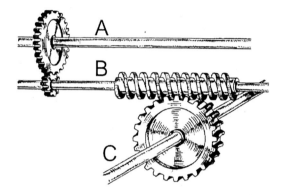

50

Which shaft can not be the driver?

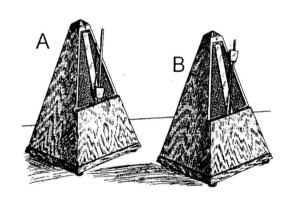

51

In which picture will the timer tick
more slowly?
(If neither, mark C.)

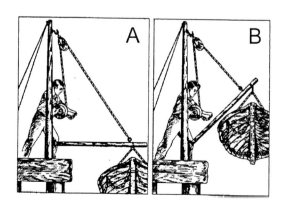

52

In which picture is it easier for the man
to turn the crank?
(If equal, mark C.)

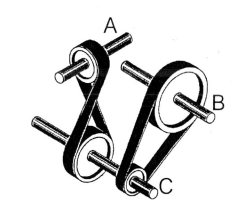

Which shaft will turn most slowly?

54

Which boy is pushing harder?
(If equal, markC.)

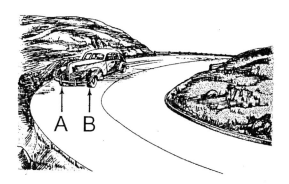

55

As this car goes around the turn, which tire presses harder on the road?
(If equal, markC.)

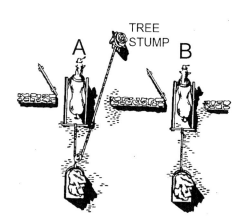

56

Which horse must walk further to pull the stone boat through the gate?
(If equal, mark C.)

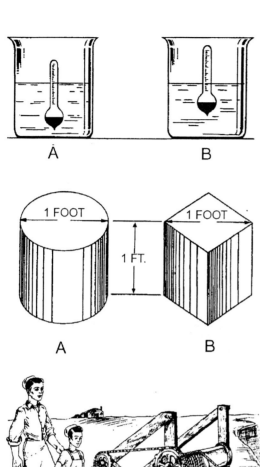

57

In which jar is the liquid lighter?
(If equal, mark C.)

58

Which weighs more?
(If equal, mark C.)

59

Which handle is better for the boy to turn?
(If either, mark C.)

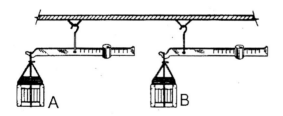

60

Which box weighs more?
(If equal, mark C.)

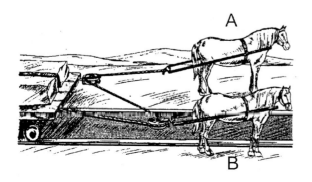

61

Which horse has to pull harder?
(If equal, mark C.)

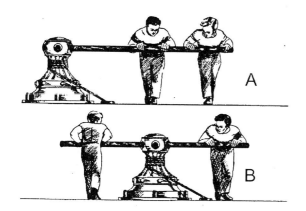

62

In which picture can the two men lift
the anchor more easily?
(If equal, mark C.)

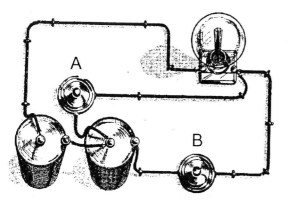

63

Which push button will make the bulb
light more brightly?
(If equal, mark C.)

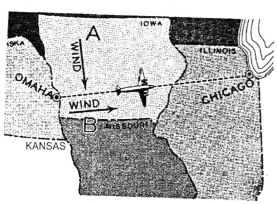

64

An airplane can make the round trip
more quickly when the wind is in
direction:
   (A) of arrow A;
   (B) of arrow B;
   (C) when there is no wind.

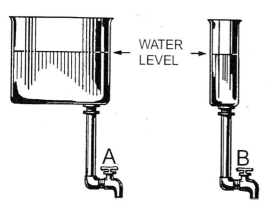

65

At which faucet is the water pressure
greater? (If equal, mark C.)

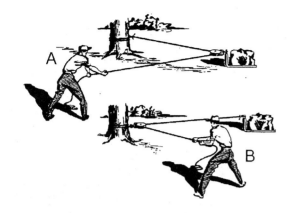

66

Which man has to pull harder?
(If equal, mark C.)

67

With which mirror can the driver see
more of what is behind him?
(If equal, mark C.)

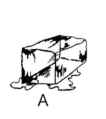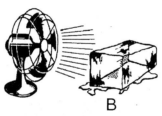

68

Which cake of ice will melt more
quickly?
(If equal, mark C.)

KEY (CORRECT ANSWERS)

1.	B	16.	A	31.	A	46.	C	61.	B
2.	A	17.	A	32.	B	47.	B	62.	B
3.	A	18.	B	33.	B	48.	C	63.	A
4.	B	19.	B	34.	B	49.	B	64.	C
5.	B	20.	B	35.	A	50.	C	65.	A
6.	B	21.	B	36.	A	51.	B	66.	A
7.	B	22.	A	37.	C	52.	B	67.	A
8.	A	23.	A	38.	A	53.	B	68.	A
9.	B	24.	B	39.	A	54.	A		
10.	B	25.	B	40.	B	55.	A		
11.	B	26.	B	41.	B	56.	A		
12.	C	27.	B	42.	B	57.	A		
13.	C	28.	C	43.	B	58.	A		
14.	A	29.	A	44.	B	59.	A		
15.	A	30.	A	45.	B	60.	B		

MECHANICAL APTITUDE
Tools and Their Use

EXAMINATION SECTION
TEST 1

DIRECTIONS : Each question or incomplete statement is followed by several suggested answers or completions. Select the one that BEST answers the question or completes the statement. *PRINT THE LETTER OF THE CORRECT ANSWER IN THE SPACE AT THE RIGHT.*

Questions 1-10.

DIRECTIONS: Questions 1 through 10 refer to the tools shown below. The numbers in the answers refer to the numbers beneath the tools.
NOTE: These tools are NOT shown to scale.

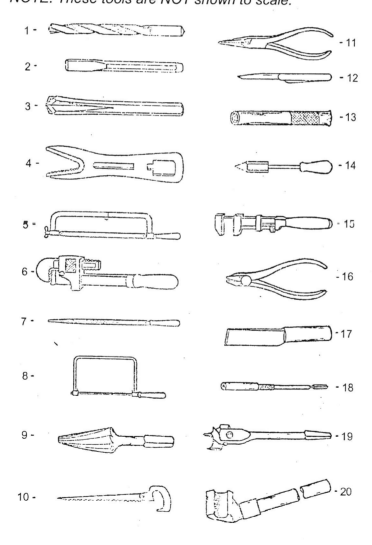

1. The tool that should be used for cutting a 1 7/8" diameter hole in a wood joist is number   1.____

    A. 3   B. 9   C. 14   D. 19

2. The tool that should be used for cutting thin-wall steel conduit is number qq   2.____

    A. 5   B. 8   C. 10   D. 16

3. The tool that should be used for soldering splices in electrical wire is number   3.____

    A. 3   B. 7   C. 13   D. 14

4. After cutting off a piece of a 3/4" diameter electrical conduit, the tool that should be used for removing a burr from the inside of the conduit is number   4.____

    A. 9   B. 11   C. 12   D. 14

5. The tool that should be used for turning a coupling onto a threaded conduit is number   5.____

    A. 6   B. 11   C. 15   D. 16

6. The tool that should be used for cutting wood lathing in plaster walls is number   6.____

    A. 5   B. 7   C. 10   D. 12

7. The tool that should be used for drilling a 3/8" diameter hole in a steel beam is number   7.____

    A. 1   B. 2   C. 3   D. 9

8. Of the following, the BEST tool to use for stripping insulation from electrical hook-up wire is number   8.____

    A. 11   B. 12   C. 15   D. 20

9. The tool that should be used for bending an electrical wire around a terminal post is number   9.____

    A. 4   B. 11   C. 15   D. 16

10. The tool that should be used for cutting electrical hook-up wire is number   10.____

    A. 5   B. 12   C. 16   D. 17

KEY (CORRECT ANSWERS)

1.	D	6.	C
2.	A	7.	A
3.	D	8.	B
4.	A	9.	B
5.	A	10.	C

TEST 2

DIRECTIONS : Each question or incomplete statement is followed by several suggested answers or completions. Select the one that BEST answers the question or completes the statement. *PRINT THE LETTER OF THE CORRECT ANSWER IN THE SPACE AT THE RIGHT.*

1. Round-nose pliers are *especially* useful for   1.____

    A. forming wire loops   B. tightening small nuts
    C. crimping wires   D. gripping small screws

2. A slight coating of rust on small tools is BEST removed by   2.____

    A. rubbing the tool with a dry cloth
    B. scraping the tool with a sharp knife
    C. scraping the tool with a small file having vaseline on it
    D. rubbing the tool with fine steel wool moistened with kerosene

3. The stake that should be used for hand-forming a small sheet metal cone is a _____ stake.   3.____

    A. hatchet   B. bottom   C. solid mandrel   D. blowhorn

4. Of the following types of pliers, the BEST one to use to clamp down sheet metal to the top of a work bench is the   4.____

    A. channel-lock   B. vise grip   C. slip-joint   D. duck bill

5. Angle brackets for supporting ductwork are *commonly* anchored to concrete walls by means of _____ bolts.   5.____

    A. carriage   B. J-   C. expansion   D. foot

6. Of the following bolts, the *one* that should be used when attaching a hanger to a wooden joist is a _____ bolt.   6.____

    A. dead   B. lag   C. dardalet   D. toggle

7. When bending sheet metal by hand, the BEST tool to use is a   7.____

    A. hand groover   B. hand seamer
    C. hand ball tooler   D. hand plier

8. Of the following types of steel rivets of the same size, the STRONGEST is the _____ rivet.   8.____

    A. tinners'   B. flathead   C. roundhead
    D. countersunk

9. Of the following snips, the one that can cut relatively thick sheet metal with the LEAST effort is _____ snips.   9.____

    A. straight   B. aviation   C. duck bill   D. hawk bill

10. Of the following, the BEST tool to use to make a hole in a concrete floor for a machine hold-down bolt is a   10.____

    A. counterboring tool   B. cold chisel
    C. drift punch   D. star drill

11. Of the following, the BEST type of saw to use to cut a 4" diameter hole through a 5/8" wooden partition is a _____ saw.   11.____

    A. back   B. saber   C. circular   D. cross-cut

12. While using a hacksaw to cut through a 1" diameter steel bar, a helper should not press down too heavily on the hacksaw because this may   12.____

    A. break the blade   B. overheat the bar
    C. permanently distort the frame
    D. cause the hacksaw to slip

13. A miter box is used   13.____

    A. for locating dowel holes in two pieces of wood to be joined together
    B. to hold a saw at a fixed angle while sawing
    C. to hold a saw while sharpening its teeth
    D. to clamp two pieces of wood together at 90 degrees

14. Wing nuts are *especially* useful on equipment where   14.____

    A. the nuts must be removed frequently and easily
    B. the nuts are locked in place with a cotter pin
    C. critical adjustments are to be made frequently
    D. a standard hex head wrench cannot be used

15. The BEST device to employ to make certain that two points, separated by an unobstructed vertical distance of 12 feet, are in the best possible vertical alignment is a   15.____

    A. carpenter's square   B. level
    C. folding ruler   D. plumb bob

16. In a shop, snips should be used to   16.____

    A. hold small parts steady while machining them
    B. cut threaded pipe
    C. cut thin gauge sheet metal
    D. remove nuts that are seized on a bolt

17. A clutch is a device that is used   17.____

    A. to hold a work piece in a fixture
    B. for retrieving small parts from hard-to-reach areas
    C. to disengage one rotating shaft from another
    D. to level machinery on a floor

18. Of the following, the BEST device to use to determine whether the surface of a work bench is horizontal is a   18.____

    A. surface gage   B. spirit level
    C. dial vernier   D. profilometer

19. Of the following, the machine screw having the SMALLEST diameter is the   19.____

    A. 10-24 x 3/4"   B. 6-32 x 1 1/4"
    C. 12-24 x 1"   D. 8-32 x 1 1/2"

20. To close off one opening in a pipe tee when the line connecting into it is to be temporarily   20.____
removed, it is necessary to use a

    A. pipe cap   B. pipe plug   C. nipple   D. bushing

21. The tool that should be used to cut a 1" x 4" plank down to a 3" width is a _____ saw.   21.____

    A. hack   B. crosscut   C. rip   D. back

22. Sharpening a hand saw consists of four major steps, *namely,*   22.____

    A. jointing, shaping, setting and filing
    B. adzing, clinching, forging and machining
    C. brazing, chiseling, grinding and mitering
    D. bushing, dressing, lapping, and machining

23. If it is necessary to shorten the length of a bolt by cutting through the threaded portion,   23.____
the SIMPLEST procedure to avoid difficulty with the thread is to

    A. cut parallel to the threads in the groove of the thread
    B. run on a die after cutting
    C. turn on a nut past the cutting point prior to cutting
    D. clear the injured thread with a 3-cornered file

24. The wrench that would prove LEAST useful in uncoupling several pieces of pipe is a   24.____
_____ wrench.

    A. socket   B. chain   C. strap   D. stillson

25. Gaskets are *commonly* used between the flanges of large pipe joints to   25.____

    A. provide space for assembly
    B. take up expansion and contraction
    C. prevent the flanges from rusting together
    D. make a tight connection

KEY (CORRECT ANSWERS)

1.	A	11.	B
2.	D	12.	A
3.	D	13.	B
4.	B	14.	A
5.	C	15.	D
6.	B	16.	C
7.	B	17.	C
8.	C	18.	B
9.	B	19.	B
10.	D	20.	B

21.	C
22.	A
23.	C
24.	A
25.	D

———

READING COMPREHENSION
UNDERSTANDING AND INTERPRETING WRITTEN MATERIAL
EXAMINATION SECTION
TEST 1

Questions 1-19.

DIRECTIONS: Each question or incomplete statement is followed by several suggested answers or completions. Select the one that BEST answers the question or completes the statement. *PRINT THE LETTER OF THE CORRECT ANSWER IN THE SPACE AT THE RIGHT.*

Questions 1-2.

DIRECTIONS: Questions 1 and 2 are to be answered on the basis of information contained in the following paragraph.

Studies show that the average high-class office building has a tenant population of around 750 persons per 100,000 square feet of area and that the elevators normally have to handle from seven to ten times as many passengers per day as the total number of permanent occupants.

1. Based on the above, what would be the AVERAGE tenant population of a building having 300,000 square feet of space?   1.____

   A. 1,000   B. 2,250   C. 2,200   D. 750

2. Based on the above, how many passengers would the elevator have to handle per day if the area of the building is 100,000 square feet?   2.____
   From

   A. 5,250 to 7,500   B. 750 to 1,500
   C. 1,000 to 2,500   D. 2,500 to 5,000

Questions 3-4.

DIRECTIONS: Questions 3 and 4 are to be answered on the basis of information contained in the following paragraph.

ELEVATOR OPERATIONS

A large number of studies show that in diversified tenancy buildings, the maximum five-minute morning incoming traffic flow averages 12% of the building population and that the noon peak at its highest five-minute period averages about 15% of the building population.

3. Based on the above, with a building population of 1,000, how many people would the elevators have to handle during the MAXIMUM incoming morning traffic period?   3.____

   A. 120   B. 130   C. 150   D. 160

4. How many people during the highest five-minute peak period of the noon rush hour would the elevator be able to handle at MAXIMUM capacity with a building population of 1,000?   4.___

    A. 120   B. 125   C. 150   D. 175

Questions 5-8.

DIRECTIONS: Questions 5 through 8 are to be answered on the basis of information contained in the following paragraph.

The speed at which an elevator should run depends upon several considerations: the height of the building, the size of the building, the purpose for which the elevator will be used, and how the elevator will be used. Elevators with extremely high speeds are of little advantage unless an express run can be established to make use of it. On local runs, by the time an elevator accelerates and then decelerates for landing, there is little time to take advantage of speed. It should also be noted that the higher the elevator speed, the larger the machine, and hence the greater the cost. Therefore, the situation must be studied before each installation and the proper speed selected to avoid the purchase of unnecessary equipment.

5. According to the above paragraph, extremely high-speed elevators are of little advantage unless   5.___

    A.   the building is small
    B.   there are only two elevators in a large building
    C.   they are used on express runs
    D.   they accelerate and decelerate slowly on local runs

6. Which one of the following is NOT mentioned in the above paragraph as a consideration in selecting the speed at which an elevator should run?   6.___

    A.   Height of the building   B.   Age of the building
    C.   Size of the building   D.   Purpose of the elevator

7. Based on the paragraph, it would be MOST correct to say that a high-speed elevator   7.___

    A.   accelerates more slowly than a low-speed elevator
    B.   uses less equipment than a low-speed elevator
    C.   breaks down more often than a low-speed elevator
    D.   costs more than a low-speed elevator

8. According to the above paragraph, one of the ways to avoid the purchase of unnecessary elevator equipment is to   8.___

    A.   study the situation before each installation
    B.   buy only low-speed elevators
    C.   use smaller machines for high-speed elevators
    D.   select low-speed elevators for express runs

Questions 9-12.

DIRECTIONS: Questions 9 through 12 are to be answered on the basis of information contained in the following paragraph.

Careful planning should always be given to the grouping of elevators in a building. When more than one elevator serves a building, the elevators should be located together as a single group or series of groups. Individual groups should be so arranged that the walking distance from the landing button to the furthermost elevator is kept at a minimum. The *alcove* arrangement, preferred for groups of five through eight elevators, has the advantage of preventing interference between people waiting for the elevators and people passing through the main corridor. It also holds *walking distance* to a minimum. The *straight line* arrangement is satisfactory for up to five cars. More than that will result in serious delays in service since the elevators must frequently wait while passengers walk from the extremities of the group.

9. According to the above paragraph, one way to prevent interference between people waiting for elevators and people using the main corridor is to   9.____

    A. use the *straight line* arrangement of elevators
    B. use the *alcove* arrangement of elevators
    C. place the landing button next to the elevator farthest from the main corridor
    D. eliminate the access from the main corridor to the elevator

10. According to the above paragraph, serious delays in elevator service may be caused by   10.____

    A. locating elevators together as a group or series of groups
    B. keeping *walking distance* to a minimum
    C. having six elevator cars in an *alcove* arrangement
    D. having seven elevator cars in a *straight line* arrangement

11. Based on the above paragraph, which of the following is the MOST accurate statement concerning the grouping of elevators in a building?   11.____

    A. The grouping of elevators always requires careful planning.
    B. Elevators should always be grouped in an *alcove* arrangement.
    C. Elevators should always be grouped in a *straight line* arrangement.
    D. A building should never contain more than eight elevators.

12. Based on the information given in the paragraph, which of the following is a PREFERRED way of arranging twelve elevator cars in a building?   12.____

    A. All twelve cars in one *alcove*
    B. All twelve cars in a *straight line*
    C. Four cars in one *alcove* and eight cars in a *straight line*
    D. Six cars in each of two *alcoves*

Questions 13-17.

DIRECTIONS: Questions 13 through 17 are to be answered on the basis of information contained in the following paragraph.

Panelboards are used to serve branch circuits to lamps, motors, elevators, or other electrical equipment. It is an *insulation* panel on which are mounted, with some degree of symmetry, various switches and circuit breakers. One *terminal* of each switch is wired to the bus bars of the panelboard; the other terminal of the switch is connected to the protective device. The bus bars of the panelboard are *energized* by a feeder which brings service to the panel from another part of the building. Panelboards are classified as flush type, service type, or by the number of wires in the feeder and branch circuit systems. Deadfront panelboards that have insulated *manually* operated main and branch breaker handles should always be used for safety reasons.

13. The word *insulated,* as used in the above paragraph, means MOST NEARLY 13.___

    A. non-conducting   B. instrument
    C. open   D. wall

14. The word *terminal,* as used in the above paragraph, means MOST NEARLY 14.___

    A. wire   B. connector   C. side   D. overload

15. The word *energized,* as used in the above paragraph, means MOST NEARLY 15.___

    A. enfolded   B. enervated
    C. receded   D. electrified

16. The word *manually,* as used in the above paragraph, means MOST NEARLY 16.___

    A. block   B. hand   C. relay   D. power

17. The number of types of classifications of panelboards is 17.___

    A. 1   B. 2   C. 3   D. 4

Questions 18-19.

DIRECTIONS: Questions 18 and 19 are to be answered on the basis of information contained in the following paragraph.

Put aside any thought of pictorial use and consider the photographic negative as a medium for recording areas of different brightness in a scene into areas of various opacities on a transparent support. Think only of brightness — forget color, tone, etc. Take brightness X as a shadow value, Y as a medium gray, and Z as a highlight; and in an imaginary scene, Y is 100 times brighter than X and Z is 100 times brighter than Y. Now take a piece of paper and rule a line for a base and another rising from this, left to right, at an angle, say 45°. At the bottom of the slanting line, put a mark X and near the top another, Z. Midway between these, put Y. You have constructed a perfect characteristic curve of an imaginary film. You can see that X, Y, and Z have the same relation to each other that they had in the scene. Running horizontal lines from these three points and measuring vertically between them, you can see the same relationship. These horizontal lines, measured to the base line, represent the densities of developed silver in the negative.

18. From the above paragraph, it is apparent that 18.___

    A. color and tone of a scene must not be overlooked
    B. brightness Z is designated as a shadow value
    C. brightness W is designated as a highlight value
    D. brightness Z is 200 times brighter than brightness A

19. From the above paragraph, we can conclude that the 19.___

    A. sloping line represents the densities of developed silver in the negative
    B. horizontal distance between points X, Y, and Z is measured along the base line

C. slanting line represents a perfect characteristic curve
D. slanting line rises from right to left

Questions 20-25.

DIRECTIONS: Each question consists of a statement. You are to indicate whether the statement is TRUE (T) or FALSE (F). *PRINT THE LETTER OF THE CORRECT ANSWER IN THE SPACE AT THE RIGHT.*

Questions 20-22.

DIRECTIONS: Questions 20 through 22 are based on the paragraph given below. Your answers to these questions must be based ONLY on the information given in this paragraph and not on any other information you may have.

Every elevator shall be given a serial number for purposes of identification. Such serial number shall be assigned when the first certificate is issued. Each borough shall keep a docket of all elevators in the borough. This docket shall give the serial number of the elevator, its location, and information as to type of construction, motive power, rise, rated speed, inspection, and such other information as the superintendent may deem desirable. The owner of the building shall cause such serial number, together with the most recent certificate of inspection, to be posted in the elevator car in the manner prescribed by the superintendent.

20. If a person knows the serial number of an elevator, he can find out the type of construction of the elevator by looking in the borough docket.   20.____

21. The purpose of the serial number is to determine which elevator was issued a certificate first.   21.____

22. The serial number of an elevator and the most recent certificate of inspection must be posted in the elevator car in the manner required by the superintendent.   22.____

Questions 23-25.

DIRECTIONS: Questions 23 through 25 are based on the paragraph given below. Your answers to these questions must be based ONLY on the information given in this paragraph and not on any other information you may have.

In selective automatic elevator operation, the elevator car will stop at each floor for which a button on the control panel is pushed. The stops occur in the order in which the floors are reached, regardless of the number of buttons that are pushed or the order in which they are pushed. Passengers may stop the elevator going in either direction by pushing the down or up buttons on their floors. The elevator will stop at these floors only if it is going in the direction of the button pushed, that is, up if the up button is pushed and down if the down button is pushed. The elevator will stop at the floors in the order in which it reaches them, stopping at all floors where up buttons are pushed on its way up and at all floors on its way down where down buttons have been pushed.

23. If the operator pushes the buttons for the fifteenth, seventeenth, eighth, and third floors in that order before he leaves the ground floor, the elevator will stop first at the third floor. 23.____

24. If passengers have pushed the down buttons on the third floor and seventh floor when the elevator has left the ground floor on its way up, the first stop will be on the third floor. 24.____

25. If the elevator is on its way up and a down button on any floor is pushed, the elevator will stop on its way up. 25.____

―――――

KEY (CORRECT ANSWERS)

1.	B	11.	A
2.	A	12.	D
3.	A	13.	A
4.	C	14.	B
5.	C	15.	D
6.	B	16.	C
7.	D	17.	B
8.	A	18.	D
9.	B	19.	C
10.	D	20.	T

21.	F
22.	T
23.	T
24.	F
25.	F

―――――

TEST 2

Questions 1-20.

DIRECTIONS: Each question or incomplete statement is followed by several suggested answers or completions. Select the one that BEST answers the question or completes the statement. *PRINT THE LETTER OF THE CORRECT ANSWER IN THE SPACE AT THE RIGHT.*

Questions 1-4.

DIRECTIONS: Questions 1 through 4 should be answered ONLY according to the information given in the following paragraph.

RELIEF PERIODS

Elevator operators will be given two (2) relief periods each day, one before and one after lunch. Relief periods will be not longer than 30 minutes and not less than 20 minutes. The number of elevator operators absent will determine the length of relief periods each day. When on relief, operators should not leave the building to which they are assigned except by permission of their supervisor.

1. Assume that your working hours on one day are from 8:15 A.M. to 5:15 P. M., with one hour off for lunch from 11:45 to 12:45.
   Relief periods which could be given to you are

   A. 9:15 to 9:45 and 11:15 to 11:45
   B. 10:15 to 10:30 and 3:30 to 4:15
   C. 10:30 to 11:00 and 2:15 to 2:40
   D. 11:30 to 12:00 and 3:00 to 3:25

   1.____

2. Suppose that three of the 15 elevator operators who normally work in your building are out sick one day. Relief periods for that day will probably be

   A. made shorter
   C. remain the same
   B. eliminated for the morning
   D. eliminated for the afternoon

   2.____

3. According to the information given in the paragraph, while on your relief period you are allowed to

   A. visit a friend in another building if you will be back before the end of your relief period
   B. buy a newspaper at the stand in the lobby of your building only with special permission of your supervisor
   C. go out of the building to buy a pack of cigarettes if you get the approval of your supervisor
   D. have coffee in the lunchroom in the building only if your relief period is more than 30 minutes

   3.____

4. Of the following, the one which is a TRUE statement according to the paragraph is   4.____

    A. an elevator operator may combine both his relief periods so that he can leave early on a day that he has to attend to personal business
    B. elevator operators can go where they wish because the relief period is their own free time
    C. relief periods may be longer than 30 minutes with the permission of the supervisor
    D. the length of the daily relief periods depends on how many elevator operators are on duty each day

Questions 5-7.

DIRECTIONS: Questions 5 through 7 should be answered ONLY according to the information given in the following paragraph.

ELEVATOR TYPES

The four kinds of power which have been used to operate elevators in buildings are hand, steam, hydraulic, and electric power. The first two types have been discarded, and hydraulic elevators are still in use only in older buildings. Electric-powered elevators are the only ones now in general use, and the very latest type have full automatic control. In general, the more nearly automatic the operation of the elevators is made, the better the performance. Power operated, center-opening doors on elevators are best, and the car doors should be solid. The center-opening door speeds passenger entrance and exit, which is an important factor in speeding service. Deep and narrow elevators are to be avoided because of loading difficulty.

5. The two types of power for operating elevators which are no longer in use are   5.____

    A. hand and hydraulic   B. hand and steam
    C. steam and hydraulic   D. hydraulic and electric

6. An advantage of center-opening doors on elevators is that such doors   6.____

    A. help in giving faster service to passengers
    B. help the operator control the speed of the elevator car
    C. prevent too many passengers from going in or out at the same time
    D. prevent accidents when passengers enter and leave the elevators

7. The BEST and LATEST type of elevator car would be   7.____

    A. deep and narrow and have electric power, automatic control, and side-opening doors
    B. wide and not too deep and have hydraulic power and center-opening doors
    C. deep and narrow and have automatic hydraulic power and center-opening doors
    D. not too deep and wide and have automatic control, electric power, and center-opening doors

Questions 8-9.

DIRECTIONS: Questions 8 and 9 are to be answered ONLY according to the information given in the following paragraph.

UNIFORMS

All operators, while on duty, must wear the standard uniform that has been adopted by the Department. Male operator's uniform consists of a cap, coat, shirt, tie, and trousers. Female operator's uniform consists of a coat, shirt, and skirt. All operators must wear black shoes. The complete uniform must be worn from September 15 to June 15. During the summer months from June 15 to September 15, the cap and coat may be omitted.

8. A CORRECT uniform to be worn during the month of December is   8._____

   A. male operator: cap, shirt, tie, trousers, and brown shoes
   B. female operator: cap, shirt, skirt, black shoes, and a sprig of holly as a Christmas decoration
   C. male operator: cap, coat, shirt, tie, trousers, and black shoes
   D. female operator: cap, coat, tie, skirt, and brown shoes

9. The summer period during which operators do not have to wear the uniform cap and coat runs from   9._____

   A. September 15th to June 15th
   B. June 15th to September 15th
   C. July 4th to Labor Day
   D. the beginning of June to the end of September

Questions 10-12.

DIRECTIONS: Questions 10 through 12 should be answered ONLY according to the information given in the following paragraph.

ACCIDENTS

In operating an elevator car, the most important rule to remember is *safety first.* In case of any accident, or on the slightest indication that anything is wrong with the operation of the car, stop the car at once at the nearest floor level and notify an immediate supervisor. In the event of an accident, however slight, obtain the names and addresses of the injured persons and of all other persons witnessing the accident. Report the accident immediately to a supervisor.

10. A passenger in the car accidentally cuts his finger on a bundle carried by another passenger. For one NOT to report this to a supervisor would be   10._____

   A. *correct* because the operator did not cause the accident
   B. *incorrect* because the operator would be relieved from duty for the rest of the day
   C. *correct* since the cut was small and did not bleed much
   D. *incorrect as* all accidents are to be reported

11. While taking up the car filled with passengers who are returning from lunch, the operator notices after the third stop that the operating controls which open and close the doors are not operating smoothly.   11._____
According to the above paragraph, it would be BEST in this situation to

A. report this to a supervisor later in the day before going off duty
B. make all required stops as the passengers would become annoyed if the operator did not get them to their floors quickly
C. get the names and addresses of all passengers
D. stop at the next floor and call a supervisor for instructions

12. When an accident happens, the operator must get the name and address of the persons injured and the name and address of the   12.___

A. supervisor on duty at the time of the accident
B. passengers who saw the accident
C. injured person's family doctor
D. hospital to which the passenger was sent for treatment

Questions 13-14.

DIRECTIONS: Questions 13 and 14 should be answered ONLY according to the information given in the following paragraph.

FLOOR BUTTONS

The floor buttons on the elevator operating panel are used to set up stops for the floors at which you want the elevator to stop. In elevators having automatic equipment, one or more of the floor buttons can be locked in the pressed position so that the elevator will stop at the same floors on each trip either up or down. To lock a floor button, press the button as you would normally, and then give it a quarter turn to the right. The button can be released by giving it a quarter turn to the left and then pulling it out of the pressed position.

13. The CORRECT and complete procedure for locking in a floor button is to   13.___

A. press in the button in the normal way
B. press the button in the usual way and give it a quarter turn in a clockwise direction
C. press in the button with a quarter turn counter-clockwise twist
D. pull out the button with a quarter turn to the left

14. If the 6th floor button on the operating panel of an automatic elevator car is kept locked in the pressed position, the car would stop at the 6th floor   14.___

A. on every up trip but not on the down trip
B. only during the morning, lunch time, and evening rush periods
C. every time the elevator comes to the floor
D. when the operator wants the elevator to stop at the 6th floor

Questions 15-20.

DIRECTIONS: Questions 15 through 20 should be answered ONLY according to the information given in the following paragraphs and diagram.

SIGNAL LIGHTS

If the elevator is one of a group that has automatic dispatching, it will have five (5) signal lights at the top of the operating panel. The following diagram shows the position, color, and the name given to each light. The main purpose of the Highest Call Return Light (amber) is to tell the

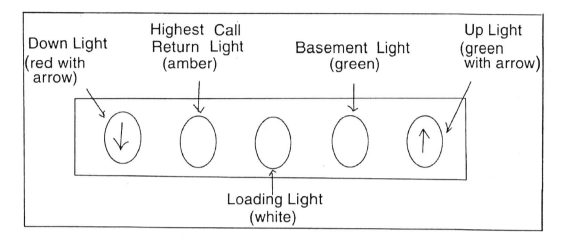

The main purpose of the Highest Call Return Light (amber) is to tell the operator when the elevator has reached its highest call. It remains lighted during up trips and goes out when the car reaches the upper floor or the top floor of the run, at which time the car will reverse.

When the car reaches the main floor, the operator should check to see if the Loading Light (white) is on. If it is not on, direct passengers to whichever car is loading. When it goes on, the operator should start taking on passengers.

When the Up Light (green) goes on, the operator should start the up trip. This light remains on until the operator reaches the top floor or the highest call.

If the Down Light (red) goes on when the car stops at a floor other than the top floor of the run, it means that the car has answered its highest call and has reversed. If the car reaches the top floor before the Down Light goes on, the operator should wait there until it goes on, and then start the down trip.

In most buildings, service to the basement is not automatic. When the car is making a down trip and there is a passenger waiting at the basement, the Basement Light (green) will go on. At this point, press the basement floor button on the operating panel which will prevent the car from automatically reversing at the main floor, and will light the Down signal instead of the Up signal over the main floor elevator entrance.

15. The two (2) signals which have the same colored lights are the _____ Light and _____ Light.
                                                  15._____

    A. Down; Up
    B. Up; Basement
    C. Basement; Highest Call Return
    D. Down; Loading

16. The operator arrives at the Main Floor, and the white light on the operating panel goes on immediately.
The operator should

    A. put the car into reverse and go to the basement
    B. immediately close the doors and start an up trip
    C. let passengers enter the elevator
    D. wait until the red light goes on and then take on passengers

16.____

17. The elevator returns to the main floor and passengers get off. No signal light is lit on the operating panel. The operator should

    A. tell passengers to take the elevator which is loading
    B. call the supervisor and tell him that the signal lights are out of order
    C. allow passengers to enter the car until the Up Light goes on
    D. go to the basement to pick up a passenger

17.____

18. During every up trip, the lights which are ALWAYS on are the

    A. Loading Light, Up Light, and Highest Call Return Light
    B. Up Light and Loading Light
    C. Loading Light and Highest Call Return Light
    D. Up Light and Highest Call Return Light

18.____

19. After the operator comes to the top floor of the run, no signal lights are lit. Before starting the down trip, the operator should wait until the

    A. white light goes on
    B. red light goes on
    C. white and red lights go on
    D. amber and white lights go on

19.____

20. While the car is on a down trip, the Basement Light (green) goes on, and the operator presses the basement floor button.
As a result, the

    A. Down signal over the main floor elevator entrance will light up
    B. elevator car will go into reverse at the main floor
    C. Highest Call Return Light (amber) will light up as the elevator car arrives at the main floor
    D. Up signal over the main floor elevator entrance will light up

20.____

Questions 21-25.

DIRECTIONS: Questions 21 through 25 are to be answered according to the information given in the following paragraph. Each question consists of a statement. You are to indicate whether the statement is TRUE (T) or FALSE (F). *PRINT THE LETTER OF THE CORRECT ANSWER IN THE SPACE AT THE RIGHT.*

No other person in a city building has as much contact with the public as the elevator operator. The operation of an elevator is an important job. The elevator operator has a chance to show the visitor to the building that city employees are helpful, efficient, and friendly. An operator should make announcements in a clear, pleasant voice and loud enough so that all passengers can hear them.

21. Other persons in a city building have more contact with the public than the elevator operator has.

21._____

22. The job of the elevator operator is an important one.

22._____

23. The elevator operator has a chance to show the visitor that city employees are helpful and friendly.

23._____

24. It isn't necessary for an elevator operator to make announcements in a pleasant voice as long as he makes them clearly.

24._____

25. An elevator operator should make announcements loud enough so that all passengers can hear them.

25._____

——————

KEY (CORRECT ANSWERS)

1.	C		11.	D
2.	A		12.	B
3.	C		13.	B
4.	D		14.	C
5.	B		15.	B
6.	A		16.	C
7.	D		17.	A
8.	C		18.	D
9.	B		19.	B
10.	D		20.	A

21.	F
22.	T
23.	T
24.	F
25.	T

——————

READING COMPREHENSION
UNDERSTANDING AND INTERPRETING WRITTEN MATERIAL
EXAMINATION SECTION
TEST 1

DIRECTIONS: Each question or incomplete statement is followed by-several suggested answers or completions. Select the one that BEST answers the question or completes the statement. *PRINT THE LETTER OF THE CORRECT ANSWER IN THE SPACE AT THE RIGHT.*

Questions 1-3.

DIRECTIONS: Questions 1 through 3, inclusive, are to be answered in accordance with the following paragraph.

All cement work contracts, more or less, in setting. The contraction in concrete walls and other structures causes fine cracks to develop at regular intervals. The tendency to contract increases in direct proportion to the quantity of cement in the concrete. A rich mixture will contract more than a lean mixture. A concrete wall which has been made of a very lean mixture and which has been built by filling only about one foot in depth of concrete in the form each day will frequently require close inspection to reveal the cracks.

1. According to the above paragraph,

    A. shrinkage seldom occurs in concrete
    B. shrinkage occurs only in certain types of concrete
    C. by placing concrete at regular intervals, shrinkage may be avoided
    D. it is impossible to prevent shrinkage

1._____

2. According to the above paragraph, the one of the factors which reduces shrinkage in concrete is the

    A. volume of concrete in wall
    B. height of each day's pour
    C. length of wall
    D. length and height of wall

2._____

3. According to the above paragraph, a rich mixture

    A. pours the easiest
    B. shows the largest amount of cracks
    C. is low in cement content
    D. need not be inspected since cracks are few

3._____

Questions 4-6.

DIRECTIONS: Questions 4 through 6, inclusive, are to be answered SOLELY on the basis of the following paragraph.

It is best to avoid surface water on freshly poured concrete in the first place. However, when there is a very small amount present, the recommended procedure is to allow it to evaporate before finishing. If there is considerable water, it is removed with a broom, belt, float, or by other convenient means. It is never good practice to sprinkle dry cement, or a mixture of cement and fine aggregate, on concrete to take up surface water. Such fine materials form a layer on the surface that is likely to dust or hair check when the concrete hardens.

4. The MAIN subject of the above passage is

    A. surface cracking of concrete
    B. evaporation of water from freshly poured concrete
    C. removing surface water from concrete
    D. final adjustments of ingredients in the concrete mix

4.____

5. According to the above passage, the sprinkling of dry cement on the surface of a concrete mix would MOST LIKELY

    A. prevent the mix from setting
    B. cause discoloration on the surface of the concrete
    C. cause the coarse aggregate to settle out too quickly
    D. cause powdering and small cracks on the surface of the concrete

5.____

6. According to the above passage, the thing to do when considerable surface water is present on the freshly poured concrete is to

    A. dump the concrete back into the mixer and drain the water
    B. allow the water to evaporate before finishing
    C. remove the water with a broom, belt, or float
    D. add more fine aggregate but not cement

6.____

Questions 7-9.

DIRECTIONS: Questions 7 through 9, inclusive, are to be answered ONLY in accordance with the information given in the paragraph below.

Before placing the concrete, check that the forms are rigid and well braced and place the concrete within 45 minutes after mixing it. Fill the forms to the top with the wearing-course concrete. Level off the surfaces with a strieboard. When the concrete becomes stiff but still workable (in a few hours), finish the surface with a wood float. This fills the hollows and compacts the concrete and produces a smooth but gritty finish. For a non-gritty and smoother surface (but one that is more slippery when wet), follow up with a steel trowel after the water sheen from the wood-troweling starts to disappear. If you wish, slant the tread forward a fraction of an inch so that it will shed rain water.

7. Slanting the tread a fraction of an inch gives a surface that will

    A. have added strength
    B. not be slippery when wet
    C. shed rain water
    D. not have hollows

7.____

8. In addition to giving a smooth but gritty finish, the use of a wood float will tend to　　8.＿＿＿

    A. give a finish that is slippery when wet
    B. compact the concrete
    C. give a better wearing course
    D. provide hollows to retain rain water

9. Which one of the following statements is most nearly correct?　　9.＿＿＿

    A. Having checked the forms, one may place the concrete immediately after mixing same.
    B. One must wait at least 15 minutes after mixing the concrete before it may be placed in the forms.
    C. A gritty compact finish and one which is more slippery when wet will result with the use of a wood float.
    D. A steel trowel used promptly after a wood float will tend to give a non-gritty smooth finish.

Questions 10-11.

DIRECTIONS: Questions 10 and 11 are to be answered SOLELY on the basis of information contained in the following paragraph.

Tools and plastering methods have changed very little over the years. Most of the changes are mere improvements of the basic tools. The tools formerly made by hand are now machine-made and are *rigidly* constructed of light, but strong, materials in contrast to the clumsy constructions of the early types. The power-driven mixers and hoisting equipment used on large plastering jobs today produce better mortars and lighten the tasks involved.

10. According to the above paragraph, present day tools used for plastering　　10.＿＿＿

    A. have made plastering much more complicated than it used to be
    B. are heavier than the old-fashioned tools they replaced
    C. produce poorer results but speed up the job
    D. are lighter and stronger than the hand-made tools of the past

11. As used in the above paragraph, the word *rigidly* means MOST NEARLY　　11.＿＿＿

    A. feeble   B. weakly   C. firmly   D. flexibly

Questions 12-18.

DIRECTIONS: Questions 12 through 18 are to be answered in accordance with the following paragraphs.

SURFACE RENEWING OVERLAYS

A surface renewing overlay should consist of material which can be constructed in very thin layers. The material must fill surface voids and provide an impervious skid-resistant surface. It must also be sufficiently resistant to traffic abrasion to provide an economical service life.

Materials meeting these requirements are:
  a. Asphalt concrete having small particle size
  b. Hot sand asphalts
  c. Surface seal coats

Fine-graded asphalt concrete or hot sand asphalt can be constructed in layers as thin as one-half inch and fulfill all requirements for surface renewing overlays. They are recommended for thin resurfacing of pavements having high traffic volumes, as their service lives are relatively long when constructed properly. They can be used for minor leveling, they are quiet riding, and their appearance is exceptionally pleasing. Seal coats or slurry seals may fulfill surface requirements for low traffic pavements.

12. A surface renewing overlay must fill surface voids, provide an impervious skid-resistant surface, and   12.___

  A. be resistant to traffic abrasion
  B. have small particle size
  C. be exceptionally pleasing in appearance
  D. be constructed in half-inch layers

13. An *impervious skid-resistant surface* means a surface that is   13.___

  A. rough to the touch and fixed firmly in place
  B. waterproof and provides good gripping for tires
  C. not damaged by skidding vehicles
  D. smooth to the touch and quiet riding

14. The number of types of materials that can be constructed in very thin layers and are also suitable for surface renewing overlays is   14.___

  A. 1   B. 2   C. 3   D. 4

15. The SMALLEST thickness of asphalt concrete or hot sand asphalt that can fulfill all requirements for surface renewing overlays is _____ inch(es).   15.___

  A. ¼   B. ½   C. 1   D. 2

16. The materials that are recommended for thin resurfacing of pavements having high traffic volumes are   16.___

  A. those that have relatively long service lives
  B. asphalt concretes with maximum particle size
  C. surface seal coats
  D. slurry seals with voids

17. Fine-graded asphalt concrete and hot sand asphalt are quiet riding and are also   17.___

  A. recommended for low traffic pavements
  B. used as slurry seal coats
  C. suitable for major leveling
  D. exceptionally pleasing in appearance

18. The materials that may fulfill surface requirements for low traffic pavements are   18._____

    A. fine-graded asphalt concretes
    B. hot sand asphalts
    C. seal coats or slurry seals
    D. those that can be used for minor leveling

Questions 19-25.

DIRECTIONS: Questions 19 through 25 are to be answered SOLELY on the basis of the paragraphs below.

OPEN-END WRENCHES

Solid, non-adjustable wrenches with openings in one or both ends are called open-end wrenches. Wrenches with small openings are usually shorter than wrenches with large openings. This proportions the lever advantage of the wrench to the bolt or stud and helps prevent wrench breakage or damage to the bolt or stud.

Open-end wrenches may have their jaws parallel to the handle or at angles anywhere up to 90 degrees. The average angle is 15 degrees. This angular displacement variation permits selection of a wrench suited for places where there is room to make only a part of a complete turn of a nut or bolt. Handles are usually straight, but may be curved. Those with curved handles are called S-wrenches. Other open-end wrenches may have offset handles. This allows the head to reach nut or bolt heads that are sunk below the surface.

There are a few basic rules that you should keep in mind when using wrenches. They are:

    I.   ALWAYS use a wrench that fits the nut properly. Otherwise, the wrench may slip, or the nut may be damaged.
    II.   Keep wrenches clean and free from oil. Otherwise, they may slip, resulting in possible serious injury to you or damage to the work.
    III.   Do NOT increase the leverage of a wrench by placing a pipe over the handle. Increased leverage may damage the wrench or the work.

19. Open-end wrenches   19._____

    A. are adjustable
    B. are solid
    C. always have openings at both ends
    D. are always S-shaped

20. Wrench proportions are such that wrenches with _____ openings have _____ handles.   20._____

    A. larger; shorter   B. smaller; longer
    C. larger; longer   D. smaller; thicker

21. The average angle between the jaws and the handle of a wrench is _____ degrees.   21._____

    A. 0   B. 15   C. 22   D. 90

22. Offset handles are intended for use MAINLY with   22.____

    A. offset nuts
    B. bolts having fine threads
    C. nuts sunk below the surface
    D. bolts that permit limited swing

23. The wrench which is selected should fit the nut properly because this   23.____

    A. prevents distorting the wrench
    B. insures use of all wrench sizes
    C. avoids damaging the nut
    D. overstresses the bolt

24. Oil on wrenches is   24.____

    A. *good* because it prevents rust
    B. *good* because it permits easier turning
    C. *bad* because the wrench may slip off the nut
    D. *bad* because the oil may spoil the work

25. Extending the handle of a wrench by slipping a piece of pipe over it is considered   25.____

    A. *good* because it insures a tight nut
    B. *good* because less effort is needed to loosen a nut
    C. *bad* because the wrench may be damaged
    D. *bad* because the amount of tightening can not be controlled

---

KEY (CORRECT ANSWERS)

1.	D	11.	C
2.	B	12.	A
3.	B	13.	B
4.	C	14.	C
5.	D	15.	B
6.	C	16.	A
7.	C	17.	D
8.	B	18.	C
9.	A	19.	B
10.	D	20.	C

21.	B
22.	C
23.	C
24.	C
25.	C

TEST 2

DIRECTIONS: Each question or incomplete statement is followed by several suggested
answers or completions. Select the one that BEST answers the question or
completes the statement. *PRINT THE LETTER OF THE CORRECT ANSWER
IN THE SPACE AT THE RIGHT.*

Questions 1-3.

DIRECTIONS: Questions 1 through 3 are to be answered SOLELY on the basis of the following passage.

A utility plan is a floor plan which shows the layout of a heating, electrical, plumbing, or
other utility system. Utility plans are used primarily by the persons reponsible for the utilities,
but they are important to the craftsman as well. Most utility installations require the leaving of
openings in walls, floors, and roofs for the admission or installation of utility features. The
craftsman who is, for example, pouring a concrete foundation wall must study the utility plans
to determine the number, sizes, and locations of the openings he must leave for piping, electric lines, and the like.

1. The one of the following items of information which is LEAST likely to be provided by a   1.____
utility plan is the

   A. location of the joists and frame members around stairwells
   B. location of the hot water supply and return piping
   C. location of light fixtures
   D. number of openings in the floor for radiators

2. According to the passage, the persons who will *most likely* have the GREATEST need for   2.____
the information included in a utility plan of a building are those who

   A. maintain and repair the heating system
   B. clean the premises
   C. paint housing exteriors
   D. advertise property for sale

3. According to the passage, a repair crew member should find it MOST helpful to consult a   3.____
utility plan when information is needed about the

   A. thickness of all doors in the structure
   B. number of electrical outlets located throughout the structure
   C. dimensions of each window in the structure
   D. length of a roof rafter

Questions 4-9.

DIRECTIONS: Questions 4 through 9 are to be answered SOLELY on the basis of the following passage.

The basic hand-operated hoisting device is the tackle or purchase, consisting of a line
called a fall, reeved through one or more blocks. To hoist a load of given size, you must set up
a rig with a safe working load equal to or in excess of the load to be hoisted. In order to do

this, you must be able to calculate the safe working load of a single part of line of given size, the safe working load of a given purchase which contains a line of given size, and the minimum size of hooks or shackles which you must use in a given type of purchase to hoist a given load. You must also be able to calculate the thrust which a given load will exert on a gin pole or a set of shears inclined at a given angle, the safe working load which a spar of a given size used as a gin pole or as one of a set of shears will sustain, and the stress which a given load will set up in the back guy of a gin pole or in the back guy of a set of shears inclined at a given angle.

4. The above passage refers to the lifting of loads by means of 　　　　4.___

    A. erected scaffolds   B. manual rigging devices
    C. power-driven equipment   D. conveyor belts

5. It can be concluded from the above passage that a set of shears serves to 　　5.___

    A. absorb the force and stress of the working load
    B. operate the tackle
    C. contain the working load
    D. compute the safe working load

6. According to the above passage, a spar can be used for a 　　　　　6.___

    A. back guy   B. block   C. fall   D. gin pole

7. According to the above passage, the rule that a user of hand-operated tackle MUST follow is to make sure that the safe working load is AT LEAST 　　7.___

    A. equal to the weight of the given load
    B. twice the combined weight of the block and falls
    C. one-half the weight of the given load
    D. twice the weight of the given load

8. According to the above passage, the two parts that make up a tackle are 　　8.___

    A. back guys and gin poles   B. blocks and falls
    C. rigs and shears   D. spars and shackles

9. According to the above passage, in order to determine whether it is safe to hoist a particular load, you MUST 　　9.___

    A. use the maximum size hooks
    B. time the speed to bring a given load to a desired place
    C. calculate the forces exerted on various types of rigs
    D. repeatedly lift and lower various loads

Questions 10-15.

DIRECTIONS: Questions 10 through 15 are to be answered SOLELY on the basis of the following set of instructions.

PATCHING SIMPLE CRACKS IN A BUILT-UP ROOF

If there is a visible crack in built-up roofing, the repair is simple and straightforward:

1. With a brush, clean all loose gravel and dust out of the crack, and clean three or four inches around all sides of it.
2. With a trowel or putty knife, fill the crack with asphalt cement and then spread a layer of asphalt cement about 1/8 inch thick over the cleaned area.
3. Place a strip of roofing felt big enough to cover the crack into the wet cement and press it down firmly.
4. Spread a second layer of cement over the strip of felt and well past its edges.
5. Brush gravel back over the patch.

10. According to the above passage, in order to patch simple cracks in a built-up roof, it is necessary to use a   10._____

    A. putty knife and a drill   B. knife and pliers
    C. tack hammer and a punch   D. brush and a trowel

11. According to the above passage, the size of the area that should be clear of loose gravel and dust before the asphalt cement is first applied should   11._____

    A. be the exact size of the crack itself
    B. extend three or four inches on all sides of the crack
    C. be 1/8 inch greater than the size of the crack itself
    D. extend the length of the roofing strip

12. According to the above passage, loose gravel and dust in the crack should be removed with a   12._____

    A. brush   B. felt pad   C. trowel   D. dust mop

13. Assume that both layers of asphalt cement needed to patch the crack are of the same thickness.   13._____
The total thickness of asphalt cement used in the patch should be MOST NEARLY _____ inch.

    A. 1/2   B. 1/3   C. 1/4   D. 1/8

14. According to the instructions in the above passage, how large should the strip of roofing felt be cut?   14._____

    A. Three of four inches square
    B. Smaller than the crack and small enough to be surrounded by cement on all sides of the strip
    C. Exactly the same size and shape of the area covered by the wet cement
    D. Large enough to completely cover the crack

15. The final or finishing action to be taken in patching a simple crack in a built-up roof is to   15._____

    A. clean out the inside of the crack
    B. spread a layer of asphalt a second time
    C. cover the crack with roofing felt
    D. cover the patch of roofing felt and cement with gravel

Questions 16-17.

DIRECTIONS: Questions 16 and 17 are to be answered SOLELY on the basis of the information given in the following paragraph.

Supplies are to be ordered from the stockroom once a week. The standard requisition form, Form SP21, is to be used for ordering all supplies. The form is prepared in triplicate, one white original and two green copies. The white and one green copy are sent to the stockroom, and the remaining green copy is to be kept by the orderer until the supplies are received.

16.   According to the above paragraph, there is a limit on the   16.___

    A.   amount of supplies that may be ordered
    B.   day on which supplies may be ordered
    C.   different kinds of supplies that may be ordered
    D.   number of times supplies may be ordered in one year

17.   According to the above paragraph, when the standard requisition form for supplies is pre-   17.___
pared,

    A.   a total of four requisition blanks is used
    B.   a white form is the original
    C.   each copy is printed in two colors
    D.   one copy is kept by the stock clerk

Questions 18-21.

DIRECTION: Questions 18 through 21 are to be answered SOLELY on the basis of the following passage.

The Oil Pollution Act for U. S. waters defines an *oily mixture* as 100 parts or more of oil in one million parts of mixture. This mixture is not allowed to be discharged into the prohibited zone. The prohibited zone may, in special cases, be extended 100 miles out to sea but, in general, remains at 50 miles offshore. The United States Coast Guard must be contacted to report all *oily mixture* spills. The Federal Water Pollution Control Act provides for a fine of $10,000 for failure to notify the United States Coast Guard. An employer may take action against an employee if the employee causes an *oily mixture* spill. The law holds your employer responsible for either cleaning up or paying for the removal of the oil spillage.

18.   According to the Oil Pollution Act, an *oily mixture* is defined as one in which there are   18.___
_____ parts or more of oil in _____ parts of mixture.

    A.   50; 10,000   B.   100; 10,000
    C.   100; 1,000,000   D.   10,000; 1,000,000

19.   Failure to notify the proper authorities of an *oily mixture* spill is punishable by a fine. Such   19.___
fine is provided for by the

    A.   United States Coast Guard
    B.   Federal Water Pollution Control Act
    C.   Oil Pollution Act
    D.   United States Department of Environmental Protection

20. According to the law, the one responsible for the removal of an *oily mixture* spilled into U.S. waters is the 20.____

    A. employer
    B. employee
    C. U.S. Coast Guard
    D. U.S. Pollution Control Board

21. The *prohibited zone,* in general, is the body of water 21.____

    A. within 50 miles offshore
    B. beyond 100 miles offshore
    C. within 10,000 yards of the coastline
    D. beyond 10,000 yards from the coastline

Questions 22-25.

DIRECTIONS: Questions 22 through 25 are to be answered SOLELY on the basis of the following paragraph.

Synthetic detergents are materials produced from petroleum products or from animal or vegetable oils and fats. One of their advantages is the fact that they can be made to meet a particular cleaning problem by altering the foaming, wetting, and emulsifying properties of a cleaner. They are added to commonly used cleaning materials such as solvents, water, and alkalies to improve their cleaning performance. The adequate wetting of the surface to be cleaned is paramount in good cleaning performance. Because of the relatively high surface tension of water, it has poor wetting ability, unless its surface tension is decreased by addition of a detergent or soap. This allows water to flow into crevices and around small particles of soil, thus loosening them.

22. According to the above paragraph, synthetic detergents are made from all of the following EXCEPT 22.____

    A. petroleum products   B. vegetable oils
    C. surface tension oils   D. animal fats

23. According to the above paragraph, water's poor wetting ability is related to 23.____

    A. its low surface tension
    B. its high surface tension
    C. its vegetable oil content
    D. the amount of dirt on the surface to be cleaned

24. According to the above paragraph, synthetic detergents are added to all of the following EXCEPT 24.____

    A. alkalines   B. water   C. acids   D. solvents

25. According to the above paragraph, altering a property of a cleaner can give an advantage in meeting a certain cleaning problem.
The one of the following that is NOT a property altered by synthetic detergents is the cleaner's

    A. flow ability
    B. foaming property
    C. emulsifying property
    D. wetting ability

25.___

———

KEY (CORRECT ANSWERS)

1.	A		11.	B
2.	A		12.	A
3.	B		13.	C
4.	B		14.	D
5.	A		15.	D
6.	D		16.	D
7.	A		17.	B
8.	B		18.	C
9.	C		19.	B
10.	D		20.	A

21.	A
22.	C
23.	B
24.	C
25.	A

———

READING COMPREHENSION
UNDERSTANDING AND INTERPRETING WRITTEN MATERIAL
EXAMINATION SECTION
TEST 1

Questions 1-10.

DIRECTIONS: Each question or incomplete statement is followed by several suggested
answers or completions. Select the one that BEST answers the question or
completes the statement. *PRINT THE LETTER OF THE CORRECT ANSWER
IN THE SPACE AT THE RIGHT.*

1. Accident prevention is an activity which depends for success upon factual information,   1.____
research, and analysis. Experience has proved that all accidents can be prevented
through the correct application of basic accident prevention methods and techniques
determined from factual cause data. Therefore, to achieve the maximum results from any
safety and health program, a uniform system for the reporting of accidents and causes is
established. The procedures required for a report, when properly carried out, will determine accurate cause factors and the most practical methods for applying preventive or
remedial action. According to the above paragraphs, which of the following statements is
MOST NEARLY correct?

   A.   No matter how much effort is put forth, there are some accidents that cannot be
prevented.
   B.   Accident prevention is a research activity.
   C.   Accident reporting systems are not related to accident prevention.
   D.   The success of an accident prevention program depends on the correct use of a
uniform accident reporting system.

Questions 2-7.

DIRECTIONS: Questions 2 through 7 are to be answered ONLY according to the information
given in the following accident report.

DATE: February 2

TO: Edward Moss, Superintendent   SUBJECT: Report of Accident to
     Pacific Houses   Philip Fay, Employee
     2487 Shell Road   1825 North 8th St.
     Auburnsville, Illinois   Auburnsville, Ill.
                                                     Identification #374-24

   Philip Fay, an employee, came to my office at 10:15 A.M. yesterday and told me that he
hurt his left elbow. When I asked him what happened, he told me that 15 minutes ago, while
shoveling the snow from in front of Building #14 at 2280 Stone Ave., he slipped on some
snow-covered ice and fell on his elbow. Joseph Sanchez and Arthur Campbell, who were
working with him, saw what happened.

Mr. Fay complained of pain and could not bend his left arm. I called for an ambulance right away. A police patrol car from the 85th Precinct arrived 15 minutes later, and Patrolman Johnson, Shield #8743, said that an ambulance was on the way. At 10:45 A.M., an ambulance arrived from Auburn Hospital. Dr. Breen examined Mr. Fay and told me that he would have to go to the hospital for some x-ray pictures to determine how bad the injury was. The ambulance left with Mr. Fay at 11:00 A.M.

At 3:45 P.M., Mr. Fay called from the hospital and told me that his arm had been put in a cast in the emergency room of the hospital. He was told that he had fractured his left elbow and would have to stay out of work for about four weeks. He is to report back at the hospital in three weeks for another examination and to see if the cast can be taken off. His wife was at the hospital with him, and they were now going home.

Attached are the statements from the witnesses and our completed REPORT OF INJURY form.

William Fields
Foreman

2. Which one of the following did NOT see the accident?   2.___

   A. Campbell   B. Fay   C. Fields   D. Sanchez

3. The CORRECT date and time of accident is February   3.___

   A. 2, 10:00 A.M.   B. 2, 10:15 A.M.
   C. 1,10:00 A.M.   D. 1, 10:15A.M.

4. The ambulance came about _____ hour after _____.   4.___

   A. 1/4 ; the accident   B. 1/4 ; it was called
   C. 1/2; the accident   D. 1/2; it was called

5. It is not possible to tell whether Fay went to report the accident right away because the   5.___
   report does NOT say

   A. how long it takes to get from Building #14 to the foreman's office
   B. how long it takes to get from Stone Ave. to Shell Rd.
   C. whether Fay telephoned the foreman first
   D. whether the foreman was in his office as soon as Fay got there

6. From the facts in the report, Fay's action might be criticized because he   6.___

   A. did not give the foreman the complete story of what had happened
   B. did not take Campbell or Sanchez with him when he went to the foreman's office in
       case he should need help on the way
   C. did not remain at the accident site and send Sanchez and Campbell to bring the
       foreman
   D. telephoned from the hospital and by using his arm to do this he might have aggra-
       vated his condition

7. Assuming that the report gives the complete story of this incident, the action of the fore-   7._____
man may be criticized because he did NOT

    A. call an ambulance soon enough
    B. go to the hospital with the ambulance and stay with the injured man until he was discharged
    C. have the injured man sign a release of claim against the department
    D. make an on-the-spot investigation of the accident scene nor take corrective action

Questions 8-10.

DIRECTIONS: Questions 8 through 10 are to be answered ONLY according to the information given in the following passage.

A foreman has four maintainers and two helpers assigned to him. Listed below are the maintainers and helpers and their rate of speed in completing the assignments given to them. Assume all the foreman's men (maintainers and helpers) are of equal technical ability but some work faster than others while some are slower in completing their assignments. In all cases, no overtime is to be granted.

    Maintainer E - works at average rate of speed
    Maintainer F - works at twice the rate of speed as Maintainer E
    Maintainer G - works at the same rate of speed as Maintainer E
    Maintainer H - works at half the rate of speed as Maintainer E
    Helper J - works at same rate of speed as Maintainer G
    Helper K - works at same rate of speed as Maintainer H

8. A certain job must be done immediately, and Maintainer H and Helper J are the only men   8._____
available.
If Maintainer F, working alone, could normally complete this job in six days, the TOTAL time this foreman should allot to Maintainer H and Helper J to complete the same job is _____ days.

    A. 3   B. 4   C. 8   D. 12

9. While Maintainer E and Helper J are working on a job, Helper J reports that he will be out   9._____
sick for at least a week. The job normally would have taken four more days to complete, and it must be completed within these four days.
If Maintainer H and Helper K are the only two men available, this foreman should

    A. assign Helper K to replace Helper J
    B. assign Maintainer H to replace Helper J
    C. assign both Maintainer H and Helper K to replace Helper J
    D. inform his assistant supervisor that the job cannot be completed on time

10. This foreman has assigned all six of his men to a routine maintenance job. At the end of   10._____
two days, the job is four-fifths completed; and instead of reassigning all his men the fol-
lowing day when they would finish early, the foreman cuts the gang so that the job will take one more full day to finish. The work gang on the last day should consist of Main-
tainer(s)

    A. F and H   B. F and Helper J
    C. E and Helpers J and K   D. G and H and Helper K

Questions 11-25.

DIRECTIONS: Each question consists of a statement. You are to indicate whether the statement is TRUE (T) or FALSE (F). *PRINT THE LETTER OF THE CORRECT ANSWER IN THE SPACE AT THE RIGHT.*

Questions 11-15.

DIRECTIONS: Questions 11 through 15 are to be answered ONLY according to the information given in the following paragraph.

USING LADDERS

All ladders must be checked each day for any defects before they are used. They should not be used if there are split rails or loose rungs or if they have become shaky. Two men should handle a stepladder which is over eight feet in height, one man if the ladder is smaller. One man must face the ladder and hold it with a firm grasp while the other is working on it. When you climb a ladder, always face it, grasp the siderails, and climb up one rung at a time. You should come down the same way.

11. A ladder which is new does not have to be inspected before it is used.   11.___

12. A ladder with a loose rung may be used if this rung is not stepped on.   12.___

13. A stepladder 6 feet long may be handled by one man.   13.___

14. If a 10-foot stepladder is used, one man must hold the ladder while the other works on it.   14.___

15. The siderails of a ladder do not have to be held when climbing down.   15.___

Questions 16-20.

DIRECTIONS: Questions 16 through 20 are to be answered ONLY according to the information given in the following paragraph.

TRAFFIC ACCIDENTS

Three auto accidents happened at the corner of Fifth Street and Seventh Avenue. The first, at 7:00 P.M. last night, knocked down a light pole when two cars collided. At 8:15 A.M. this morning, two other autos crashed head on. This afternoon, at 12:30 P.M., another pair of cars crashed. One of them jumped the curb, knocked over two traffic signs, and damaged three parked cars at the corner service station. No serious injury to the drivers was reported, but all the cars involved were severely damaged.

16. Nine cars were damaged in the three accidents.   16.___

17. The three accidents happened within a period of 14 hours.   17.___

18. A service station is located at the corner of Fifth Street and Seventh Avenue.   18.___

10. In the last accident, both cars jumped the curb and knocked over two light poles.   19.___

20. The drivers of the cars in the last accident were badly hurt.   20.___

Questions 21-25.

DIRECTIONS: Questions 21 through 25 are to be answered ONLY according to the information given in the following paragraph.

<u>LIFTING</u>

Improper lifting of heavy objects is a frequent cause of strains and ruptures. When a heavy object is to be lifted, an employee should stand close to the object and face it squarely. The feet are spread slightly apart, and one foot is a little ahead of the other. Then, bend the knees to bring the body down to the object and keep your back comfortably vertical. Raise the object slightly to see if you can lift it alone. If you can, get a firm grasp with both hands, balance the object, and raise it by straightening the legs, but still keeping the back erect. The raising motion is gradual, not swift. In this way you use the leg muscles which are the strongest muscles in the body. This method of lifting prevents strain to the back muscles which are weak and not built for lifting purposes.

21. Many ruptures are the result of not lifting heavy objects in the correct manner.   21.____

22. When an employee lifts a heavy package, he should keep his feet close together in order to balance the load.   22.____

23. When lifting a heavy object, the back should not be bent but kept upright.   23.____

24. It is best to lift heavy objects quickly in order to prevent strains and ruptures.   24.____

25. For purposes of lifting, the leg muscles are stronger than the arm muscles.   25.____

KEY (CORRECT ANSWERS)

1.	D	11.	F
2.	C	12.	F
3.	C	13.	T
4.	D	14.	T
5.	A	15.	F
6.	B	16.	T
7.	D	17.	F
8.	C	18.	T
9.	C	19.	F
10.	B	20.	F

21. T
22. F
23. T
24. F
25. T

TEST 2

Questions 1-8.

DIRECTIONS: Questions 1 through 8, inclusive, are based on the ladder safety rules given below. Read these rules fully before answering these questions.

LADDER SAFETY RULES

When a ladder is placed on a slightly uneven supporting surface, use a flat piece of board or small wedge to even up the ladder feet. To secure the proper angle for resting a ladder, it should be placed so that the distance from the base of the ladder to the supporting wall is one-quarter the length of the ladder. To avoid overloading a ladder, only one person should work on a ladder at a time. Do not place a ladder in front of a door. When the top rung of a ladder rests against a pole, the ladder should be lashed securely. Clear loose stones or debris from the ground around the base of a ladder before climbing. While on a ladder, do not attempt to lean so that any part of the body, except arms or hands, extends more than 12 inches beyond the side rail. Always face the ladder when ascending or descending. When carrying ladders through buildings, watch for ceiling globes and lighting fixtures. Avoid the use of rolling ladders as scaffold supports.

1. A small wedge is used to   1.___

   A. even up the feet of a ladder resting on an uneven surface
   B. lock the wheels of a roller ladder
   C. secure the proper resting angle for a ladder
   D. secure a ladder against a pole

2. An 8-foot ladder resting against a wall should be so inclined that the distance between   2.___
   the base of the ladder and the wall is _____ feet.

   A. 2   B. 5   C. 7   D. 9

3. A ladder should be lashed securely when   3.___

   A. it is placed in front of a door
   B. loose stones are on the ground near the base of the ladder
   C. the top rung rests against a pole
   D. two people are working from the same ladder

4. Rolling ladders   4.___

   A. should be used for scaffold supports
   B. should not be used for scaffold supports
   C. are useful on uneven ground
   D. should be used against a pole

5. When carrying a ladder through a building, it is necessary to   5._____

    A. have two men to carry it
    B. carry the ladder vertically
    C. watch for ceiling globes
    D. face the ladder while carrying it

6. It is POOR practice to   6._____

    A. lash a ladder securely at any time
    B. clear debris from the base of a ladder before climbing
    C. even up the feet of a ladder resting on slightly uneven ground
    D. place a ladder in front of a door

7. A person on a ladder should NOT extend his head beyond the side rail by more than   7._____
    _____ inches.

    A. 12   B. 9   C. 7   D. 5

8. The MOST important reason for permitting only one person to work on a ladder at a time   8._____
    is that

    A. both could not face the ladder at one time
    B. the ladder will be overloaded
    C. time would be lost going up and down the ladder
    D. they would obstruct each other

Questions 9-13.

DIRECTIONS: Questions 9 through 13 concern an excerpt of written material which you are
              to read and study carefully. The excerpt is immediately followed by five state-
              ments which refer to it alone. You are required to judge whether each state-
              ment
              A. is entirely true
              B. is entirely false
              C. is partly true and partly false
              D. may or may not be true but cannot be answered on the basis of
                  the facts as given in the excerpt

      It is true that in 1987 there were more strikes than in any year, excepting 1986, since
1970. However, the number of workers involved was less in 1987 than in any year since 1981,
and man-days of idleness due to strikes, the MOST accurate measure of industrial strife,
were less in 1987 than in any year since 1980, again excepting 1986.

9.   There were fewer workers involved in strikes in 1986 than in 1981.   9._____

10. There were more strikes in 1986 than in 1987.   10._____

11. There were more strikes in 1986 than in 1970.   11._____

12. There were fewer workers involved in strikes but more man days of idleness in 1981 than   12._____
     1987.

13. There were fewer man-days of idleness and fewer workers involved in strikes in 1986 than 1987.　　13.___

Questions 14-16.

DIRECTIONS: Questions 14 through 16 are to be answered on the basis of the information given in the following passage.

Telephone service in a government agency should be adequate and complete with respect to information given or action taken. It must be remembered that telephone contacts should receive special consideration since the caller cannot see the operator. People like to feel that they are receiving personal attention and that their requests or criticisms are receiving individual rather than routine consideration. All this contributes to what has come to be known as Tone of Service. The aim is to use standards which are clearly very good or superior. The factors to be considered in determining what makes good Tone of Service are speech, courtesy, understanding, and explanations. A caller's impression of Tone of Service will affect the general attitude toward the agency and city services in general.

14. The above passage states that people who telephone a government agency like to feel that they are　　14.___

    A. creating a positive image of themselves
    B. being given routine consideration
    C. receiving individual attention
    D. setting standards for telephone service

15. Which of the following is NOT mentioned in the above passage as a factor in determining good Tone of Service?　　15.___

    A. Courtesy
    C. Speech
    B. Education
    D. Understanding

16. The above passage IMPLIES that failure to properly handle telephone calls is *most likely* to result in　　16.___

    A. a poor impression of city agencies by the public
    B. a deterioration of courtesy toward operators
    C. an effort by operators to improve the Tone of Service
    D. special consideration by the public of operator difficulties

Questions 17-20.

DIRECTIONS: Questions 17 through 20 are to be answered ONLY according to the information given in the following passage.

ACCIDENT PREVENTION

Many accidents and injuries can be prevented if employees learn to be more careful. The wearing of shoes with thin or badly worn soles or open toes can easily lead to foot injuries from tacks, nails, and chair and desk legs. Loose or torn clothing should not be worn near moving machinery. This is especially true of neckties which can very easily become caught in the machine. You should not place objects so that they block or partly block hallways, corridors, or other passageways. Even when they are stored in the proper place, tools, supplies, and equipment should be carefully placed or piled so as not to fall, nor have anything stick out from a pile. Before cabinets, lockers or ladders are moved, the tops should be cleared of anything which might injure someone or fall off. If necessary, use a dolly to move these or other bulky objects.

Despite all efforts to avoid accidents and injuries, however, some will happen. If an employee is injured, no matter how small the injury, he should report it to his supervisor and have the injury treated. A small cut that is not attended to can easily become infected and can cause more trouble than some injuries which at first seem more serious. It never pays to take chances.

17. According to the above passage, the one statement that is NOT true is that   17._____

    A. by being more careful, employees can reduce the number of accidents that happen
    B. women should wear shoes with open toes for comfort when working
    C. supplies should be piled so that nothing is sticking out from the pile
    D. if an employee sprains his wrist at work, he should tell his supervisor about it

18. According to the above passage, you should NOT wear loose clothing when you are   18._____

    A. in a corridor   B. storing tools
    C. opening cabinets   D. near moving machinery

19. According to the above passage, before moving a ladder you should   19._____

    A. test all the rungs
    B. get a dolly to carry the ladder at all times
    C. remove everything from the top of the ladder which might fall off
    D. remove your necktie

20. According to the above passage, an employee who gets a slight cut should   20._____

    A. have it treated to help prevent infection
    B. know that a slight cut becomes more easily infected than a big cut
    C. pay no attention to it as it can't become serious
    D. realize that it is more serious than any other type of injury

Questions 21-24.

DIRECTIONS: Questions 21 through 24 are to be answered on the basis of the following report.

TO: Thomas Smith   Date: June 14.
        Supervising Menagerie Keeper

                                        Subject:

FROM: Jay Jones
        Senior Menagerie Keeper

On June 14, a visitor to the monkey house at the zoo was noticed annoying the animals. He was frightening the animals by making loud noises and throwing stones at the animals in the cages. The visitor was asked to stop annoying the animals but did not. And he was then asked to leave the monkey house by the keeper on duty. The visitor would not leave and said that the zoo is public property and that as a citizen he has every right to be there. The keeper kept trying to pursuade the visitor to leave but was unsuccessful. The keeper finally threatened to call the police. The visitor soon left the monkey house and did not return. Fortunately, no animals were harmed in this incident.

21. The subject of the report has been left out.
Which one of these would be the BEST statement for the subject of the report?

    A. Loud noises in the monkey house
    B. Police called to monkey house
    C. Visitor annoying monkeys on June 14
    D. Monkeys unharmed by visitor

21.____

22. Which one of these is an important piece of information that should have been included in the FIRST sentence of the report?

    A. The kinds of monkeys in the monkey house
    B. Whether the visitor was a man or a woman
    C. The address of the monkey house
    D. The name of the zoo where the incident took place

22.____

23. The fourth sentence which begins with the words *And he was then asked...* is poorly written because

    A. the sentence begins with *And*
    B. the words *monkey house* should be written *Monkey House*
    C. the words *on duty* should be written *on-duty*
    D. *didn't* would be better than *did not*

23.____

24. In the sixth sentence, which begins with the words *The keeper kept trying...* , a word that is spelled wrong is

    A. trying   B. pursuade
    C. visitor   D. unsuccessful

24.____

Questions 25-27.

DIRECTIONS: Questions 25 through 27 test how well you can read and understand what you read. Read about ELEPHANTS. Then, on the basis of what you read, answer these questions.

ELEPHANTS

Elephants are peaceful animals and have very few real natural enemies. As with many other animals, when faced with danger the elephant tries to make himself look larger to his enemy. He does this by raising his head and trunk to look taller. The elephant will also extend his ears to look wider. Other threatening gestures may be made. The elephant may shift his weight from side to side, make a shrill scream, or pretend to charge with his trunk held high. If the enemy still fails to retreat, the elephant will make a serious attack.

25. When an elephant is in danger, he tries to make it appear that he is

    A. stronger   B. smaller   C. larger   D. angry

25.____

26. When he is threatened, an elephant tries to make himself look broader by 26.____

    A. taking a deep breath
    B. spreading out his ears
    C. shifting his weight from side to side
    D. holding his trunk high

27. If his enemy does not run away, the elephant will 27.____

    A. attack him
    B. run in the opposite direction
    C. hit the enemy with his trunk
    D. make a shrill scream

Questions 28-30.

DIRECTIONS: Read about PREVENTING DISEASE. Then, on the basis of what you read, answer Questions 28 through 30.

PREVENTING DISEASE

Proper feeding, housing, and handling are important in maintaining an animal's defenses against disease and parasites. The best diets are those that contain proteins, vitamins, minerals, and the other essential food elements. Proteins are especially important because they are necessary for growth. Minerals such as iron, copper, and cobalt help correct anemia. It has been shown that an animal's resistance can be decreased by improper feeding. However, it has not been proved that the use of certain types of feeds will increase the resistance of animals to infectious diseases. If animals are kept in good condition by proper diet and sanitary conditions, natural resistance to disease and parasites will be highest.

28. Food elements that are required especially for growth are 28.____

    A. minerals   B. vitamins
    C. proteins   D. carbohydrates

29. If animals are NOT fed correctly, they will 29.____

    A. have more diseases
    B. fight with each other
    C. need more proteins
    D. be able to kill parasites

30. The bodies of animals will BEST be able to fight disease naturally when they 30.____

    A. are kept warm
    B. are given immunity shots
    C. are given extra food
    D. have good diet and clean quarters

KEY (CORRECT ANSWERS)

1.	A		16.	A
2.	A		17.	B
3.	C		18.	D
4.	B		19.	C
5.	C		20.	A
6.	D		21.	C
7.	A		22.	D
8.	B		23.	A
9.	B		24.	B
10.	A		25.	C
11.	D		26.	B
12.	A		27.	A
13.	C		28.	C
14.	C		29.	A
15.	B		30.	D

ARITHMETIC

EXAMINATION SECTION
TEST 1

DIRECTIONS: Each question or incomplete statement is followed by several suggested answers or completions. Select the one that BEST answers the question or completes the statement. *PRINT THE LETTER OF THE CORRECT ANSWER IN THE SPACE AT THE RIGHT.*

1. The sum of 76342 + 49050 + 21206 + 59989 is   1._____
   - A. 196586
   - B. 206087
   - C. 206587
   - D. 234487

2. The sum of $452.13 + $963.83 + $621.25 is   2._____
   - A. $1936.83
   - B. $2037.21
   - C. $2095.73
   - D. $2135.73

3. The sum of 36392 + 42156 + 98765 is   3._____
   - A. 167214
   - B. 177203
   - C. 177313
   - D. 178213

4. The sum of 40125 + 87123 + 24689 is   4._____
   - A. 141827
   - B. 151827
   - C. 151937
   - D. 161947

5. The sum of 2379 + 4015 + 6521 + 9986 is   5._____
   - A. 22901
   - B. 22819
   - C. 21801
   - D. 21791

6. From 50962 subtract 36197. The answer should be   6._____
   - A. 14675
   - B. 14765
   - C. 14865
   - D. 24765

7. From 90000 subtract 31920. The answer should be   7._____
   - A. 58072
   - B. 59062
   - C. 68172
   - D. 69182

8. From 63764 subtract 21548. The answer should be   8._____
   - A. 42216
   - B. 43122
   - C. 45126
   - D. 85312

9. From $9605.13 subtract $2715.96. The answer should be   9._____
   - A. $12,321.09
   - B. $8,690.16
   - C. $6,990.07
   - D. $6,889.17

10. From 76421 subtract 73101. The answer should be   10._____
    - A. 3642
    - B. 3540
    - C. 3320
    - D. 3242

11. From $8.25 subtract $6.50. The answer should be   11._____
    - A. $1.25
    - B. $1.50
    - C. $1.75
    - D. $2.25

12. Multiply 563 by 0.50. The answer should be   12._____
    - A. 281.50
    - B. 28.15
    - C. 2.815
    - D. 0.2815

13. Multiply 0.35 by 1045. The answer should be   13.____
   A. 0.36575   B. 3.6575   C. 36.575   D. 365.75

14. Multiply 25 by 2513. The answer should be   14.____
   A. 62825   B. 62725   C. 60825   D. 52825

15. Multiply 423 by 0.01. The answer should be   15.____
   A. 0.0423   B. 0.423   C. 4.23   D. 42.3

16. Multiply 6.70 by 3.2. The answer should be   16.____
   A. 2.1440   B. 21.440   C. 214.40   D. 2144.0

17. Multiply 630 by 517. The answer should be   17.____
   A. 325,710   B. 345,720   C. 362,425   D. 385,660

18. Multiply 35 by 846. The answer should be   18.____
   A. 4050   B. 9450   C. 18740   D. 29610

19. Multiply 823 by 0.05. The answer should be   19.____
   A. 0.4115   B. 4.115   C. 41.15   D. 411.50

20. Multiply 1690 by 0.10. The answer should be   20.____
   A. 0.169   B. 1.69   C. 16.90   D. 169.0

21. Divide 2765 by 35. The answer should be   21.____
   A. 71   B. 79   C. 87   D. 93

22. From $18.55 subtract $6.80. The answer should be   22.____
   A. $9.75   B. $10.95   C. $11.75   D. $25.35

23. The sum of 2.75 + 4.50 + 3.60 is   23.____
   A. 9.75   B. 10.85   C. 11.15   D. 11.95

24. The sum of 9.63 + 11.21 + 17.25 is   24.____
   A. 36.09   B. 38.09   C. 39.92   D. 41.22

25. The sum of 112.0 + 16.9 + 3.84 is   25.____
   A. 129.3   B. 132.74   C. 136.48   D. 167.3

KEY (CORRECT ANSWERS)

1.	C	11.	C
2.	B	12.	A
3.	C	13.	D
4.	C	14.	A
5.	A	15.	C
6.	B	16.	B
7.	A	17.	A
8.	A	18.	D
9.	D	19.	C
10.	C	20.	D

21.	B
22.	C
23.	B
24.	B
25.	B

SOLUTIONS TO PROBLEMS

1. 76,342 + 49,050 + 21,206 + 59,989 = 206,587

2. $452.13 + $963.83 + $621.25 = $2037.21

3. 36,392 + 42,156 + 98,765 = 177,313

4. 40,125 + 87,123 + 24,689 = 151,937

5. 2379 + 4015 + 6521 + 9986 = 22901

6. 50,962 - 36,197 = 14,765

7. 90,000 - 31,928 = 58,072

8. 63,764 - 21,548 = 42,216

9. $9605.13 - $2715.96 = $6889.17

10. 76,421 - 73,101 = 3320

11. $8.25 - $6.50 = $1.75

12. (563)(.50) = 281.50

13. (.35)(1045) = 365.75

14. (25)(2513) = 62,825

15. (423)(.01) = 4.23

16. (6.70)(3.2) = 21.44

17. (630)(517) = 325,710

18. (35)(846) = 29,610

19. (823)(.05) = 41.15

20. (1690)(.10) = 169

21. 2765 ÷ 35 = 79

22. $18.55 - $6.80 = $11.75

23. 2.75 + 4.50 + 3.60 = 10.85

24. 9.63 + 11.21 + 17.25 = 38.09

25. 112.0 + 16.9 + 3.84 = 132.74

TEST 2

Questions 1-10.

DIRECTIONS: Questions 1 through 10 refer to the arithmetic examples shown in the boxes below. Be sure to refer to the proper box when answering each question.

23.3 - 5.72	$491.26 -127.47	$7.95 ÷ $0.15	4758 1639 2075 864 23	27.6 179.47 8.73 46.5
BOX 1	BOX 2	BOX 3	BOX 4	BOX 5
243 x57	57697 -9748	23.65 x 9.7	3/4 260	25/1975
BOX 6	BOX 7	BOX 8	BOX 9	BOX 10

1. The difference between the two numbers in Box 1 is   1.____

   A. 17.42   B. 17.58   C. 23.35   D. 29.02

2. The difference between the two numbers in Box 2 is   2.____

   A. $274.73   B. $363.79   C. $374.89   D. $618.73

3. The result of the division indicated in Box 3 is   3.____

   A. $0.53   B. $5.30   C. 5.3   D. 53

4. The sum of the five numbers in Box 4 is   4.____

   A. 8355   B. 9359   C. 9534   D. 10359

5. The sum of the four numbers in Box 5 is   5.____

   A. 262.30   B. 272.03   C. 372.23   D. 372.30

6. The product of the two numbers in Box 6 is   6.____

   A. 138.51   B. 1385.1   C. 13851   D. 138510

7. The difference between the two numbers in Box 7 is   7.____

   A. 67445   B. 48949   C. 47949   D. 40945

8. The product of the two numbers in Box 8 is   8.____

   A. 22.9405   B. 229.405   C. 2294.05   D. 229405

9. The product of the two numbers in Box 9 is   9.____

   A. 65   B. 120   C. 195   D. 240

10. The result of the division indicated in Box 10 is

    A. 790   B. 379   C. 179   D. 79

10.____

Questions 11-20.

DIRECTIONS: Questions 11 through 20 refer to the arithmetic examples shown in the boxes below. Be sure to refer to the proper box when answering each question.

BOX 1	BOX 2	BOX 3	BOX 4	BOX 5
3849 728 3164 773 32	18.70 268.38 17.64 9.40	66788 -8639	154 x48	32.56 x 8.6

BOX 6	BOX 7	BOX 8	BOX 9	BOX 10
34/2890	32.49 - 8.7	$582.17 -38.58	$6.72 ÷ $0.24	3/8 x 264

11. The sum of the five numbers in Box 1 is

    A. 7465   B. 7566   C. 8465   D. 8546

11.____

12. The sum of the four numbers in Box 2 is

    A. 341.21   B. 341.12   C. 314.21   D. 314.12

12.____

13. The difference between the two numbers in Box 3 is

    A. 75427   B. 74527   C. 58149   D. 57149

13.____

14. The product of the two numbers in Box 4 is

    A. 1232   B. 6160   C. 7392   D. 8392

14.____

15. The product of the two numbers in Box 5 is

    A. 28.016   B. 280.016   C. 280.16   D. 2800.16

15.____

16. The result of the division indicated in Box 6 is

    A. 85   B. 850   C. 8.5   D. 185

16.____

17. The difference between the two numbers in Box 7 is

    A. 23.79   B. 21.53   C. 19.97   D. 18.79

17.____

18. The difference between the two numbers in Box 8 is

    A. $620.75   B. $602.59   C. $554.75   D. $543.59

18.____

19. The result of the division indicated in Box 9 is

    A. .0357   B. 28.0   C. 280   D. 35.7

19.____

20. The product of the two numbers in Box 10 is

    A. 9.90   B. 89.0   C. 99.0   D. 199.

20.____

21. When 2597 is added to the result of 257 multiplied by 65, the answer is

    A. 16705   B. 19302   C. 19392   D. 19402

21.____

22. When 948 is subtracted from the sum of 6527 + 324, the answer is

    A. 5255   B. 5903   C. 7151   D. 7799

22.____

23. When 736 is subtracted from the sum of 3191 + 1253, the answer is

    A. 2674   B. 3708   C. 4444   D. 5180

23.____

24. Divide 6 2/3 by 2 1/2.

    A. 2 2/3   B. 16 2/3   C. 3 1/3   D. 2 1/2

24.____

25. Add: 1/2 + 2 1/4 + 2/3

    A. 3 1/4   B. 2 7/8   C. 4 1/4   D. 3 5/12

25.____

KEY (CORRECT ANSWERS)

1.	B		11.	D
2.	B		12.	D
3.	D		13.	C
4.	B		14.	C
5.	A		15.	B
6.	C		16.	A
7.	C		17.	A
8.	B		18.	D
9.	C		19.	B
10.	D		20.	C

21. B
22. B
23. B
24. A
25. D

SOLUTIONS TO PROBLEMS

1. 23.3 - 5.72 = 17.58

2. $491.26 - $127.47 = $363.79

3. $7.95 $.15 = 53

4. 4758 + 1639 + 2075 + 864 + 23 = 9359

5. 27.6 + 179.47 + 8.73 + 46.5 = 262.3

6. (243)(57) = 13,851

7. 57,697 - 9748 = 47,949

8. (23.65X9.7) = 229.405

9. $(\frac{3}{4})(260) = 195$

10. 1975 ÷ 25 = 79

11. 3849 + 728 + 3164 + 773 + 32 = 8546

12. 18.70 + 268.38 + 17.64 + 9.40 = 314.12

13. 66,788 - 8639 = 58,149

14. (154)(48) = 7392

15. (32.56)(8.6) = 280.016

16. 2890 34 = 85

17. 32.49 - 8.7 = 23.79

18. $582.17 - $38.58 = $543.59

19. $6.72 ÷ $.24 = 28

20. $(\frac{3}{8})(264) = 99$

21. 2607 ı (257)(65) ⹀ 2507 ı 10,705 – 19,002

22. (6527 + 324) - 948 = 6851 - 948 = 5903

23. (3191 + 1253) - 736 = 4444 - 736 = 3708

24. $6\frac{2}{3} \div 2\frac{1}{2} = (\frac{20}{3})(\frac{2}{5}) = \frac{40}{15} = 2\frac{2}{3}$

25. $\frac{1}{2} + 2\frac{1}{4} + \frac{2}{3} = \frac{6}{12} + 2\frac{3}{12} + \frac{8}{12} = 2\frac{17}{12} = 3\frac{5}{12}$

TEST 3

Questions 1-10.

DIRECTIONS: Questions 1 through 10 refer to the arithmetic examples shown in the boxes below. Be sure to refer to the proper box when answering each item.

8462 2974 5109 763 47	14/1890	182 x63	27412 -8426	$275.15 -162.28
BOX 1	BOX 2	BOX 3	BOX 4	BOX 5
2/3 x 246	14.36 x 7.2	14.6 9.22 143.18 27.1	$6.45 ÷ $0.15	16.6 - 7.91
BOX 6	BOX 7	BOX 8	BOX 9	BOX 10

1. The sum of the five numbers in Box 1 is   1.____

    A. 16245   B. 16355   C. 17245   D. 17355

2. The result of the division indicated in Box 2 is   2.____

    A. 140   B. 135   C. 127 6/7   D. 125

3. The product of the two numbers in Box 3 is   3.____

    A. 55692   B. 16552   C. 11466   D. 1638

4. The difference between the two numbers in Box 4 is   4.____

    A. 18986   B. 19096   C. 35838   D. 38986

5. The difference between the two numbers in Box 5 is   5.____

    A. $103.87   B. $112.87   C. $113.97   D. $212.87

6. The product of the two numbers in Box 6 is   6.____

    A. 82   B. 123   C. 164   D. 369

7. The product of the two numbers in Box 7 is   7.____

    A. 103.492   B. 103.392   C. 102.392   D. 102.292

8. The sum of the four numbers in Box 8 is   8.____

    A. 183.00   B. 183.10   C. 194.10   D. 204.00

9. The result of the division indicated in Box 9 is   9.____

    A. $0.43   B. 4.3   C. 43   D. $4.30

10. The difference between the two numbers in Box 10 is   10.____

    A. 8.69   B. 8.11   C. 6.25   D. 3.75

11. Add $4.34, $34.50, $6.00, $101.76, and $90.67. From the result, subtract $60.54 and   11.____
$10.56.

    A. $76.17   B. $156.37   C. $166.17   D. $300.37

12. Add 2,200, 2,600, 252, and 47.96. From the result, subtract 202.70, 1,200, 2,150, and   12.____
434.43.

    A. 1,112.83   B. 1,213.46   C. 1,341.51   D. 1,348.91

13. Multiply 1850 by .05 and multiply 3300 by .08. Then, add both results.   13.____

    A. 242.50   B. 264.00   C. 333.25   D. 356.50

14. Multiply 312.77 by .04. Round off the result to the nearest hundredth.   14.____

    A. 12.52   B. 12.511   C. 12.518   D. 12.51

15. Add 362.05, 91.13, 347.81, and 17.46. Then, divide the result by 6.   15.____
The answer rounded off to the nearest hundredth is

    A. 138.409   B. 137.409   C. 136.41   D. 136.40

16. Add 66.25 and 15.06. Then, multiply the result by 2 1/6. The answer is MOST NEARLY   16.____

    A. 176.18   B. 176.17   C. 162.66   D. 162.62

17. Each of the following options contains three decimals. In which case do all three deci-   17.____
mals have the same value?

    A. .3; .30; .03   D. .25; .250; .2500
    C. 1.9; 1.90; 1.09   D. .35; .350; .035

18. Add 1/2 the sum of (539.84 and 479.26) to 1/3 the sum of (1461.93 and 927.27). Round   18.____
off the result to the nearest whole number.

    A. 3408   B. 2899   C. 1816   D. 1306

19. Multiply $5,906.09 by 15%. Then, divide the result by 3.   19.____

    A. $295.30   B. $885.91   C. $8,859.14   D. $29,530.45

20. A team has won 10 games, lost 4, and has 6 games yet to play.   20.____
How many of these remaining games MUST be won if the team is to win 65% of its
games for the season?

    A. One   B. Two
    C. Four   D. None of the above

21. If a certain candy sells at the rate of $1 for 2 1/2 ounces, what is the price per pound?   21.____
(Do not include tax.)

    A. $2.50   B. $6.40   C. $8.50   D. $1.00

22. Which is the SMALLEST of the following numbers?   22.____

   A. .3980   B. .3976   C. .39752   D. .399

23. A tank can be filled by one pipe in 10 minutes and by another in 15 minutes.   23.____
How long will it take to fill the tank if both pipes are opened?
_____ min.

   A. 4   B. 5   C. 6   D. 7.5

24. If $17.60 is to be divided between two people so that one person receives one and three-   24.____
fourths as much as the other, how much should each receive?

   A. $6.40 and $11.20   B. $5.50 and $12.10
   C. $6.60 and $11.20   D. $6.00 and $11.60

25. Mr. Burns owns a block of land which is exactly 320 ft. long and 140 ft. wide.   25.____
At 40¢ per square foot, how much will it cost to build a 4 foot cement walk around this
land, bound by its outer edge?

   A. $1420.80   B. $1472   C. $368   D. $1446.40

KEY (CORRECT ANSWERS)

1. D	11. C
2. B	12. A
3. C	13. D
4. A	14. D
5. B	15. C
6. C	16. B
7. B	17. B
8. C	18. D
9. C	19. A
10. A	20. D

21. B
22. C
23. C
24. A
25. D

SOLUTIONS TO PROBLEMS

1. 8462 + 2974 + 5109 + 763 + 47 = 17,355

2. 1890 ÷ 14 = 135

3. (182)(63) = 11,466

4. 27,412 - 8426 = 18,986

5. $275.15 - $162.28 = $112.87

6. $(\frac{2}{3})(246) = 164$

7. (14.36)(7.2) = 103.392

8. 14.6 + 9.22 + 143.18 + 27.1 = 194.1

9. $6.45 $.15 = 43

10. 16.6 - 7.91 = 8.69

11. ($4.34 + $34.50 + $6.00 + $101.76 + $90.67) - ($60.54 + $10.56) = $237.27 - $71.10 = $166.17

12. (2200 + 2600 + 252 + 47.96) - (202.70 + 1200 + 2150 + 434.43) = 5099.96 - 3987.13 = 1112.83

13. (1850)(.05) + (3300X.08) = 92.5 + 264 = 356.5

14. (312.77)(.04) = 12.5108 = 12.51 rounded off to nearest hundredth

15. (362.05 + 91.13 + 347.81 + 17.46) 6 = 818.45 6 = 136.4083" = 136.41 rounded off to nearest hundredth

16. $(66.25+15.06)(2\frac{1}{6}) = (81.31)(2\frac{1}{6}) \approx 176.17$

17. .25 = .250 = .2500

18. 1/2(539.84 + 479.26) + 1/3(1461.93 + 927.27) = 509.55 + 796.4 = 1305.95 = 1306 rounaed off to nearest whole number

19. $(\$5906.09)(.15)(\frac{1}{3}) = \$295.3045 = \$295.30$ rounded off to 2 places

20. (.65)(20) = 13 games won. Thus, the team must win 3 more games.

21. Let x = price per pound. Then, $\dfrac{1.00}{x} = \dfrac{2\frac{1}{2}}{16}$. Solving, x = 6.40

22. .39752 is the smallest of the numbers.

23. Let x = required minutes. Then, $\dfrac{x}{10} + \dfrac{x}{15} = 1$. So, 3x + 2x = 30. Solving, x = 6.

24. Let x, 1.75x represent the two amounts. Then, x + 1.75x = $17.60. Solving, x = $6.40 and 1.75x = $11.20.

25. Area of cement walk = (320)(140) - (312)(132) = 3616 sq.ft. Then, (3616)(.40) = $1446.40.

TEST 4

DIRECTIONS: Each question or incomplete statement is followed by several suggested answers or completions. Select the one that BEST answers the question or completes the statement. *PRINT THE LETTER OF THE CORRECT ANSWER IN THE SPACE AT THE RIGHT.*

1. Subtract: 10,376
    -8,492   1.____

    A. 1834   B. 1884   C. 1924   D. 2084

2. Subtract: $155.22
    - 93.75   2.____

    A. $61.47   B. $59.33   C. $59.17   D. $58.53

3. Subtract: $22.50
    -13.78   3.____

    A. $9.32   B. $9.18   C. $8.92   D. $8.72

4. Multiply: 485
    x32   4.____

    A. 13,350   B. 15,520   C. 16,510   D. 17,630

5. Multiply: $3.29
    x 14   5.____

    A. $41.16   B. $42.46   C. $44.76   D. $46.06

6. Multiply: 106
    x318   6.____

    A. 33,708   B. 33,632   C. 33,614   D. 33,548

7. Multiply: 119
    x1.15   7.____

    A. 136.85   B. 136.94   C. 137.15   D. 137.34

8. Divide: 432 by 16   8.____

    A. 37   B. 32   C. 27   D. 24

9. Divide: $115.65 by 5   9.____

    A. $24.25   B. $23.13   C. $22.83   D. $22.55

10. Divide: 18,711 by 63   10.____

    A. 267   B. 273   C. 283   D. 297

11. Divide: 327.45 by .15   11.____

    A. 1,218   B. 2,183   C. 2,243   D. 2,285

12. The sum of 637.894, 8352.16, 4.8673, and 301.5 is MOST NEARLY   12.____
   A. 8989.5   B. 9021.35   C. 9294.9   D. 9296.4

13. If 30 is divided by .06, the result is   13.____
   A. 5   B. 50   C. 500   D. 5000

14. The sum of the fractions 1/3, 4/6, 3/4, 1/2, and 1/12 is   14.____
   A. 3 1/4   B. 2 1/3   C. 2 1/6   D. 1 11/12

15. If 96934.42 is divided by 53.496, the result is MOST NEARLY   15.____
   A. 181   B. 552   C. 1812   D. 5520

16. If 25% of a number is 48, the number is   16.____
   A. 12   B. 60   C. 144   D. 192

17. The average number of reports filed per day by a clerk during a five-day week was 720.   17.____
   He filed 610 reports the first day, 720 reports the second day, 740 reports the third day,
   and 755 reports the fourth day.
   The number of reports he filed the fifth day was
   A. 748   B. 165   C. 775   D. 565

18. The number 88 is 2/5 of   18.____
   A. 123   B. 141   C. 220   D. 440

19. If the product of 8.3 multiplied by .42 is subtracted from the product of 156 multiplied by   19.____
   .09, the result is MOST NEARLY
   A. 10.6   B. 13.7   C. 17.5   D. 20.8

20. The sum of 284.5, 3016.24, 8.9736, and 94.15 is MOST NEARLY   20.____
   A. 3402.9   B. 3403.0   C. 3403.9   D. 4036.1

21. If 8394.6 is divided by 29.17, the result is MOST NEARLY   21.____
   A. 288   B. 347   C. 2880   D. 3470

22. If two numbers are multiplied together, the result is 3752. If one of the two numbers is 56,   22.____
   the other number is
   A. 41   B. 15   C. 109   D. 67

23. The sum of the fractions 1/4, 2/3, 3/8, 5/6, and 3/4 is   23.____
   A. 20/33   B. 1 19/24   C. 2 1/4   D. 2 7/8

24. The fraction 7/16 expressed as a decimal is   24.____
   A. .1120   B. .2286   C. .4375   D. .4850

25. If .10 is divided by 50, the result is   25.____
   A. .002   B. .02   C. .2   D. 2

KEY (CORRECT ANSWERS)

1.	B		11.	B
2.	A		12.	D
3.	D		13.	C
4.	B		14.	B
5.	D		15.	C
6.	A		16.	D
7.	A		17.	C
8.	C		18.	C
9.	B		19.	A
10.	D		20.	C

21.	A
22.	D
23.	D
24.	C
25.	A

———

SOLUTIONS TO PROBLEMS

1. 10,376 - 8492 = 1884

2. $155.22 - $93.75 = $61.47

3. $22.50 - $13.78 = $8.72

4. (485)(32) = 15,520

5. ($3.29)(14) = $46.06

6. (106)(318) = 33,708

7. (119)(1.15) = 136.85

8. 432 ÷ 16 = 27

9. $115.65÷5=$23.13

10. 18,711÷63=297

11. 327.45 ÷ .15 = 2183

12. 637.894 + 8352.16 + 4.8673 + 301.5 = 9296.4213 ≈ 9296.4

13. 30 ÷ .06 = 500

14. $\frac{1}{3}+\frac{4}{6}+\frac{3}{4}+\frac{1}{2}+\frac{1}{12}=\frac{4}{12}+\frac{8}{12}+\frac{9}{12}+\frac{6}{12}+\frac{1}{12}=\frac{28}{12}=2\frac{1}{3}$

15. 96,934.42 ÷ 53.496 ≈ 1811.99 ≈ 1812

16. Let x = number. Then, .25x = 48. Solving, x = 192.

17. Let x = number of reports on 5th day. Then, (610 + 720 + 740 + 755 + x)/5 = 720. Simplifying, 2825 + x = 3600, so x = 775.

18. $88÷\frac{2}{5}=220$

19. (156)(.09) - (8.3)(.42) = 10.554 ≈ 10.6

20. 284.5 + 3016.24 + 8.9736 + 94.15 = 3403.8636 ≈ 3403.9

21. $8394.6 \div 29.17 \approx 287.78 \approx 288$

22.   The other number = $3752 \div 56 = 67$

23. $\dfrac{1}{4}+\dfrac{2}{3}+\dfrac{3}{8}+\dfrac{5}{6}+\dfrac{3}{4}=\dfrac{6}{24}+\dfrac{16}{24}+\dfrac{9}{24}+\dfrac{20}{24}+\dfrac{18}{24}=\dfrac{69}{24}=2\dfrac{7}{8}$

24. $\dfrac{7}{16}=.4375$

25. $.10 \div 50 = .002$

———

ARITHMETIC

EXAMINATION SECTION
TEST 1

DIRECTIONS: Each question or incomplete statement is followed by several suggested answers or completions. Select the one that BEST answers the question or completes the statement. *PRINT THE LETTER OF THE CORRECT ANSWER IN THE SPACE AT THE RIGHT.*

1. From 30983 subtract 29998. The answer should be

    A.   985   B.   995   C.   1005   D.   1015

1.____

2. From $2537.75 subtract $1764.28. The answer should be

    A. $763.58   B. $773.47   C. $774.48   D. $873.58

2.____

3. From 254211 subtract 76348. The answer should be

    A.   177863   B.   177963   C.   187963   D.   188973

3.____

4. Divide 4025 by 35. The answer should be

    A.   105   B.   109   C.   115   D.   125

4.____

5. Multiply 0.35 by 2764. The answer should be

    A.   997.50   B.   967.40   C.   957.40   D.   834.40

5.____

6. Multiply 1367 by 0.50. The answer should be

    A.   6.8350   B.   68.350   C.   683.50   D.   6835.0

6.____

7. Multiply 841 by 0.01. The answer should be

    A.   0.841   B.   8.41   C.   84.1   D.   841

7.____

8. Multiply 1962 by 25. The answer should be

    A.   47740   B.   48460   C.   48950   D.   49050

8.____

9. Multiply 905 by 0.05. The answer should be

    A.   452.5   B.   45.25   C.   4.525   D.   0.4525

9.____

10. Multiply 8.93 by 4.7. The answer should be

    A.   41.971   B.   40.871   C.   4.1971   D.   4.0871

10.____

11. Multiply 25 by 763. The answer should be

    A.   18075   B.   18875   C.   19075   D.   20965

11.____

12. Multiply 2530 by 0.10. The answer should be

    A.   2.5300   B.   25.300   C.   253.00   D.   2530.0

12.____

13. Multiply 3053 by 0.25. The answer should be   13.____

     A. 76.325   B. 86.315   C. 763.25   D. 863.15

14. Multiply 6204 by 0.35. The answer should be   14.____

     A. 2282.40   B. 2171.40   C. 228.24   D. 217.14

15. Multiply $.35 by 7619. The answer should be   15.____

     A. $2324.75   B. $2565.65   C. $2666.65   D. $2756.75

16. Multiply 6513 by 45. The answer should be   16.____

     A. 293185   B. 293085   C. 292185   D. 270975

17. Multiply 3579 by 70. The answer should be   17.____

     A. 25053.0   B. 240530   C. 250530   D. 259530

18. A class had an average of 24 words correct on a spelling test. The class average on this   18.____
spelling test was 80%.
The AVERAGE number of words missed on this test was

     A. 2   B. 4   C. 6   D. 8

19. In which one of the following is 24 renamed as a product of primes?   19.____

     A. 2 x 6 x 2   B. 8 x 3 x 1
     C. 2 x 2 x 3 x 2   D. 3 x 4 x 2

Questions 20-23.

DIRECTIONS: In answering Questions 20 through 23, perform the indicated operation. Select the BEST answer from the choices below.

20. Add: 7068   20.____
            2807
            9434
            6179

     A. 26,488   B. 24,588   C. 25,488   D. 25,478

21. Divide: $75\sqrt{45555}$ 21.____

     A. 674   B. 607.4   C. 6074   D. 60.74

22. Multiply: 907   22.____
               x806

     A. 73,142   B. 13,202   C. 721,042   D. 731,042

23. Subtract: 60085   23.____
              -47194

     A. 12,891   B. 13,891   C. 12,991   D. 12,871

24. A librarian reported that 1/5% of all books taken out last school year had not been returned.
    If 85,000 books were borrowed from the library, how many were not returned?

    A. 170   B. 425   C. 1,700   D. 4,250

    24.____

25. At 40 miles per hour, how many minutes would it take to travel 12 miles?

    A. 30   B. 18   C. 15   D. 20

    25.____

KEY (CORRECT ANSWERS)

1.	A		11.	C
2.	B		12.	C
3.	A		13.	C
4.	C		14.	B
5.	B		15.	C
6.	C		16.	B
7.	B		17.	C
8.	D		18.	C
9.	B		19.	C
10.	A		20.	C

21. B
22. D
23. A
24. A
25. B

SOLUTIONS TO PROBLEMS

1. 30,983 - 29,998 = 985

2. $2537.75 - $1764.28 = $773.47

3. 254,211 - 76,348 = 177,863

4. 4025 ÷ 35 = 115

5. (.35)(2764) = 967.4

6. (1367)(.50) = 683.5

7. (841)(.01) = 8.41

8. (1962)(25) = 49,050

9. (905)(.05) = 45.25

10. (8.93)(4.7) = 41.971

11. (25)(763) = 19,075

12. (2530)(.10) = 253

13. (3053)(.25) = 763.25

14. (6204)(.35) = 2171.4

15. ($.35)(7619) = $2666.65

16. (6513)(45) = 293,085

17. (3579)(70) = 250,530

18. 24 ÷ .80 = 30. Then, 30 - 24 = 6 words

19. 24 = 2 x 2 x 3 x 2, where each number is a prime.

20. 7068 ÷ 2807 + 9434 + 6179 = 25,488

21. 45,555 ÷ 75 = 607.4

22. (907)(806) = 731,042

23. 60,085 - 47,194 = 12,891

24. (1/5%)(85,000) = (.002)(85,000) = 170 books

25. Let x = number of minutes. Then, $\frac{40}{60} = \frac{12}{x}$. Solving, x = 18

TEST 2

DIRECTIONS: Each question or incomplete statement is followed by several suggested answers or completions. Select the one that BEST answers the question or completes the statement. *PRINT THE LETTER OF THE CORRECT ANSWER IN THE SPACE AT THE RIGHT.*

1. The sum of 57901 + 34762 is

   A. 81663   B. 82663   C. 91663   D. 92663

1.____

2. The sum of 559 + 448 + 362 + 662 is

   A. 2121   B. 2031   C. 2021   D. 1931

2.____

3. The sum of 36153 + 28624 + 81379 is

   A. 136156   B. 146046   C. 146146   D. 146156

3.____

4. The sum of 742 + 9197 + 8972 is

   A. 19901   B. 18911   C. 18801   D. 17921

4.____

5. The sum of 7989 + 8759 + 2726 is

   A. 18455   B. 18475   C. 19464   D. 19474

5.____

6. The sum of $111.55 + $95.05 + $38.80 is

   A. $234.40   B. $235.30   C. $245.40   D. $254.50

6.____

7. The sum of 1302 + 46187 + 92610 + 4522 is

   A. 144621   B. 143511   C. 134621   D. 134521

7.____

8. The sum of 47953 + 58041 + 63022 + 22333 is

   A. 170248   B. 181349   C. 191349   D. 200359

8.____

9. The sum of 76563 + 43693 + 38521 + 50987 + 72723 is

   A. 271378   B. 282386   C. 282487   D. 292597

9.____

10. The sum of 85923 + 97211 + 11333 + 4412 + 22533 is

   A. 209302   B. 212422   C. 221412   D. 221533

10.____

11. The sum of 4299 + 54163 + 89765 + 1012 + 38962 is

   A. 188201   B. 188300   C. 188301   D. 189311

11.____

12. The sum of 48526 + 709 + 11534 + 80432 + 6096 is

   A. 135177   B. 139297   C. 147297   D. 149197

12.____

13. The sum of $407.62 + $109.01 + $68.44 + $378.68 is

   A. $963.75   B. $964.85   C. $973.65   D. $974.85

13.____

14. From 40614 subtract 4697. The answer should be   14._____

    A.   35917   B.   35927   C.   36023   D.   36027

15. From 81773 subtract 5717. The answer should be   15._____

    A.   75964   B.   76056   C.   76066   D.   76956

16. From $1755.35 subtract $1201.75. The answer should be   16._____

    A. $542.50   B. $544.50   C. $553.60   D. $554.60

17. From $2402.10 subtract $998.85. The answer should be   17._____

    A. $1514.35   B. $1504.25   C. $1413.25   D. $1403.25

18. Add: 12 1/2   18._____
              2 1/2
              3 1/2

    A.   17   B.   17 1/4   C.   17 3/4   D.   18

19. Subtract: 150   19._____
              -80

    A.   70   B.   80   C.   130   D.   150

20. After cleaning up some lots in the city dump, five cleanup crews loaded the following   20._____
amounts of garbage on trucks:
    Crew No. 1 loaded 2 1/4 tons
    Crew No. 2 loaded 3 tons
    Crew No. 3 loaded 1 1/4 tons
    Crew No. 4 loaded 2 1/4tons
    Crew No. 5 loaded 1/2 ton.
The TOTAL number of tons of garbage loaded was .

    A.   8 1/4   B.   8 3/4   C.   9   D.   9 1/4

21. Subtract: 17 3/4   21._____
            -7 1/4

    A.   7 1/2   B.   10 1/2   C.   14 1/4   D.   17 3/4

22. Yesterday, Tom and Bill each received 10 leaflets about rat control. They were supposed   22._____
to distribute one leaflet to each supermarket in the neighborhood. When the day was
over, Tom had 8 leaflets left. Bill had no leaflets left.
How many supermarkets got leaflets yesterday?

    A.   8   B.   10   C.   12   D.   18

23. What is 2/3 of 1 1/8?   23._____

    A.   1 11/16   B.   3/4   C.   3/8   D.   4 1/3

24. A farmer bought a load of 120 bushels of corn.   24._____
After he fed 45 bushels to his hogs, what fraction of his supply remained?

    A.   5/8   B.   3/5   C.   3/8   D.   4/7

25. In the numeral 3,159,217, the 2 is in the _____ column.   25._____

    A. hundreds   B. units   C. thousands   D. tens

KEY (CORRECT ANSWERS)

1.	D	11.	A
2.	B	12.	C
3.	D	13.	A
4.	B	14.	A
5.	D	15.	B
6.	C	16.	C
7.	A	17.	D
8.	C	18.	D
9.	C	19.	A
10.	C	20.	D

21.	B
22.	C
23.	B
24.	A
25.	A

SOLUTIONS TO PROBLEMS

1. $57,901 + 34,762 = 92,663$

2. $559 + 448 + 362 + 662 = 2031$

3. $36,153 + 28,624 + 81,379 = 146,156$

4. $742 + 9197 + 8972 = 18,911$

5. $7989 + 8759 + 2726 = 19,474$

6. $\$111.55 + \$95.05 + \$38.80 = \$245.40$

7. $1302 + 46,187 + 92,610 + 4522 = 144,621$

8. $47,953 + 58,041 + 63,022 + 22,333 = 191,349$

9. $76,563 + 45,693 + 38,521 + 50,987 + 72,723 = 282,487$

10. $85,923 + 97,211 + 11,333 + 4412 + 22,533 = 221,412$

11. $4299 + 54,163 + 89,765 + 1012 + 38,962 = 188,201$

12. $48,526 + 709 + 11,534 + 80,432 + 6096 = 147,297$

13. $\$407.62 + \$109.01 + \$68.44 + \$378.68 = \$963.75$

14. $40,614 - 4697 = 35,917$

15. $81,773 - 5717 = 76,056$

16. $\$1755.35 - \$1201.75 = \$553.60$

17. $\$2402.10 - \$998.85 = \$1403.25$

18. $12\ 1/2 + 2\ 1/4 + 3\ 1/4 = 17\ 4/4 = 18$

19. $150 - 80 = 70$

20. $2\ 1/4 + 3 + 1\ 1/4 + 2\ 1/4 + 1/2 = 8\ 5/4 = 9\ 1/4$ tons

21. $17\ 3/4 - 7\ 1/4 = 10\ 2/4 = 10\ 1/2$

22. $10 + 10 - 8 - 0 = 12$ supermarkets

23. $(\frac{2}{3})(1\frac{1}{8}) = (\frac{2}{3})(\frac{9}{8}) = \frac{18}{24} = \frac{3}{4}$

24. $120 - 45 = 75$. Then, $\frac{75}{120} = \frac{5}{8}$

25. The number 2 is in the hundreds column of 3,159,217

TEST 3

DIRECTIONS: Each question or incomplete statement is followed by several suggested answers or completions. Select the one that BEST answers the question or completes the statement. *PRINT THE LETTER OF THE CORRECT ANSWER IN THE SPACE AT THE RIGHT.*

1. The distance covered in three minutes by a subway train traveling at 30 mph is _____ mile(s). 1.____

   A. 3   B. 2   C. 1 1/2   D. 1

2. A crate contains 3 pieces of equipment weighing 73, 84, and 47 pounds, respectively. 2.____
   The empty crate weighs 16 pounds.
   If the crate is lifted by 4 trackmen, each trackman lifting one corner of the crate, the AVERAGE number of pounds lifted by each of the trackmen is

   A. 68   B. 61   C. 55   D. 51

3. The weight per foot of a length of square-bar 4" x 4" in cross-section, as compared with 3.____
   one 2" x 2" in cross-section, is _____ as much.

   A. twice   B. 2 1/2 times
   C. 3 times   D. 4 times

4. An order for 360 feet of 2" x 8" lumber is shipped in 20-foot lengths. 4.____
   The MAXIMUM number of 9-foot pieces that can be cut from this shipment is

   A. 54   B. 40   C. 36   D. 18

5. If a trackman gets $10.40 per hour and time and one-half for working over 40 hours, his 5.____
   gross salary for a week in which he worked 44 hours should be

   A. $457.60   B. $478.40   C. $499.20   D. $514.80

6. If a section of ballast 6'-0" wide, 8'-0" long, and 2'-6" deep is excavated, the amount of 6.____
   ballast removed is _____ cu. feet.

   A. 96   B. 104   C. 120   D. 144

7. The sum of 7'2 3/4", 0'-2 7/8", 3'-0", 4'-6 3/8", and 1'-9 1/4" is 7.____

   A. 16'-8 1/4"   B. 16'-8 3/4"   C. 16'-9 1/4"   D. 16' -9 3/4"

8. The sum of 3 1/16", 4 1/4", 2 5/8", and 5 7/16" is 8.____

   A. 15 3/16"   B. 15 1/4"   C. 15 3/8"   D. 15 1/2"

9. Add: $51.79, $29.39, and $8.98. 9.____
   The CORRECT answer is

   A. $78.97   B. $88.96   C. $89.06   D. $90.16

10. Add: $72.07 and $31.54. Then subtract $25.75. 10.____
    The CORRECT answer is

    A. $77.86   B. $82.14   C. $88.96   D. $129.36

11. Start with $82.47. Then subtract $25.50, $4.75, and 35¢.
The CORRECT answer is   11._____

    A. $30.60   B. $51.87   C. $52.22   D. $65.25

12. Add: $19.35 and $37.75. Then subtract $9.90 and $19.80.
The CORRECT answer is   12._____

    A. $27.40   B. $37.00   C. $37.30   D. $47.20

13. Add: $153   13._____
             114
             210
         +186

    A. $657   B. $663   C. $713   D. $757

14. Add: $64.91   14._____
          13.53
          19.27
         20.00
       +72.84

    A. $170.25   B. $178.35   C. $180.45   D. $190.55

15. Add: 1963   15._____
          1742
       +2497

    A. 6202   B. 6022   C. 5212   D. 5102

16. Add: 206   16._____
          709
       1342
      +2076

    A. 3432   B. 3443   C. 4312   D. 4333

17. Subtract: $190.76   17._____
         -    .99

    A. $189.97   B. $189.87   C. $189.77   D. $189.67

18. From 99876 subtract 85397. The answer should be   18._____

    A. 14589   B. 14521   C. 14479   D. 13589

19. From $876.51 subtract $92.89. The answer should be   19._____

    A. $773.52   B. $774.72   C. $783.62   D. $784.72

20. From 70935 subtract 49489. The answer should be   20._____

    A. 20436   B. 21446   C. 21536   D. 21546

21. From $391.55 subtract $273.45. The answer should be

    A. $118.10   B. $128.20   C. $178.10   D. $218.20

22. When 119 is subtracted from the sum of 2016 + 1634, the answer is

    A. 2460   B. 3531   C. 3650   D. 3769

23. Multiply 35 x 65 x 15. The answer should be

    A. 2275   B. 24265   C. 31145   D. 34125

24. Multiply: 4.06
                 x.031

    A. 1.2586   B. .12586   C. .02586   D. .1786

25. When 65 is added to the result of 14 multiplied by 13, the answer is

    A. 92   B. 182   C. 247   D. 16055

21._____
22._____
23._____
24._____
25._____

KEY (CORRECT ANSWERS)

1. C	11. B	
2. C	12. A	
3. D	13. B	
4. C	14. D	
5. B	15. A	
6. C	16. D	
7. C	17. C	
8. C	18. C	
9. D	19. C	
10. A	20. B	

21. A
22. B
23. D
24. B
25. C

SOLUTIONS TO PROBLEMS

1. Let x = distance. Then, $\dfrac{30}{60} = \dfrac{x}{3}$ Solving, x = 1 1/2 miles

2. $(73 + 84 + 47 + 16) \div 4 = 55$ pounds

3. $(4 \times 4) \div (2 \times 2) =$ a ratio of 4 to 1.

4. $20 \div 9 = 2\ 2/9$, rounded down to 2 pieces. Then, $(360 \div 20)(2) = 36$

5. Salary $=(\$10.40)(40) + (\$15.60)(4) = \$478.40$

6. $(6)(8)(2\ 1/2) = 120$ cu.ft.

7. $7'2\dfrac{3}{4}" + 0'2\dfrac{7}{8}" + 3'0" + 4'6\dfrac{3}{8}" + 1'9\dfrac{1}{4}" = 15'19\dfrac{18}{8}" = 15'21\dfrac{1}{4}" = 16'9\dfrac{1}{4}"$

8. $3\dfrac{1}{16}" + 4\dfrac{1}{4}" + 2\dfrac{5}{8}" + 5\dfrac{7}{16}" = 14\dfrac{22}{16}" = 15\dfrac{3}{8}"$

9. $\$51.79 + \$29.39 + \$8.98 = \$90.16$

10. $\$72.07 + \$31.54 = \$103.61$. Then, $\$103.61 - \$25.75 = \$77.86$

11. $\$82.47 - \$25.50 - \$4.75 - \$0.35 = \$51.87$

12. $\$19.35 + \$37.75 = \$57.10$. Then, $\$57.10 - \$9.90 - \$19.80 = \$27.40$

13. $\$153 + \$114 + \$210 + \$186 = \$663$

14. $\$64.91 + \$13.53 + \$19.27 + \$20.00 + \$72.84 = \$190.55$

15. $1963 + 1742 + 2497 = 6202$

16. $206 + 709 + 1342 + 2076 = 4333$

17. $\$190.76 - .99 = \$189.77$

18. $99,876 - 85,397 = 14,479$

19. $\$876.51 - \$92.89 = \$783.62$

20. $70,935 - 49,489 = 21,446$

21. $\$391.55 - \$273.45 = \$118.10$

22. $(2016 + 1634) - 119 = 3650 - 119 = 3531$

23. $(35)(65)(15) = 34,125$

24. $(4.06)(.031) = .12586$

25. $65 + (14)(13) = 65 + 182 = 247$

――――

ARITHMETIC

EXAMINATION SECTION
TEST 1

DIRECTIONS: Each question or incomplete statement is followed by several suggested answers or completions. Select the one that BEST answers the question or completes the statement. *PRINT THE LETTER OF THE CORRECT ANSWER IN THE SPACE AT THE RIGHT.*

1. 575 x 269 =   1.____

    A. 156,475   B. 154,765
    C. 154,675   D. none of the above

2. 837 x 720 =   2.____

    A. 602,640   B. 602,460
    C. 620,460   D. none of the above

3. 414 x 961 =   3.____

    A. 397,854   B. 397,845
    C. 397,485   D. none of the above

4. 898 x 303 =   4.____

    A. 272,049   B. 272,904
    C. 272,194   D. none of the above

5. 5,623 x 2,183 =   5.____

    A. 12,275,099   B. 12,275,009
    C. 12,276,009   D. none of the above

6. 913.67 x 1.04 =   6.____

    A. 950.1628   B. 9502.168
    C. 950.2168   D. none of the above

7. 313 x 2.78 =   7.____

    A. 870.41   B. 870.14
    C. 870.10   D. none of the above

8.   69   8.____
      23
      12
    +14

    A. 117   B. 118
    C. 120   D. none of the above

9.   318   9.____
     902
      45
    +18

    A. 1,228   B. 1,282
    C. 1,828   D. none of the above

10. $ 78.50
   .65
118.20
  7.07

  A. $204.42   B. $214.43
  C. $214.42   D. none of the above

11. 8.6809
  .7516
+ 1.5403

  A. 10.9787   B. 10.9738
  C. 10.9728   D. none of the above

12. 53
781
 60
+199

  A. 1,003   B. 1,099
  C. 1,093   D. none of the above

13. 6 1/8
 4 2/3
+9 1/6

  A. 19 23/24   B. 20 11/12
  C. 19 21/24   D. none of the above

14. 2 1/2
 8 1/4
+7 1/6

  A. 17 5/6   B. 17 11/13
  C. 18 1/12   D. none of the above

15. $ 463.57
 -84.68

  A. $378.88   B. $388.89
  C. $378.89   D. none of the above

16. $ 1,682.40
 -834.12

  A. $848.82   B. $848.22
  C. $884.28   D. none of the above

17. 991.17
-916.68

  A. 74.99   B. 74.49
  C. 79.99   D. none of the above

18. 6,241
   - 861

   18._____

   A. 5,480
   C. 5,408
   B. 5,380
   D. none of the above

19.   8971.6
   - 333.3

   19._____

   A. 8648.3
   C. 8683.3
   B. 8638.3
   D. none of the above

20.   39 1/4
   - 7 1/2

   20._____

   A. 31 1/2
   C. 30 1/2
   B. 31 3/4
   D. none of the above

21. $6\sqrt{5052}$ =

   21._____

   A. 842
   C. 844
   B. 804
   D. none of the above

22. $12\sqrt{7596}$ =

   22._____

   A. 630
   C. 636
   B. 603
   D. none of the above

23. $14\sqrt{368.501}$ =

   23._____

   A. 26.3251
   C. 26.3215
   B. 25.3255
   D. none of the above

24. $21\sqrt{391.73}$ =

   24._____

   A. 18.654 (approximately)
   C. 18.635 (approximately)
   B. 18.653 (approximately)
   D. none of the above

25. $5\cdot4\sqrt{175.5}$ =

   25._____

   A. 325.4
   C. 33.55
   B. 32.45
   D. none of the above

26. $2\sqrt{8\ 3/8}$ =

   26._____

   A. 4 7/16
   C. 4 3/16
   B. 4 3/4
   D. none of the above

27. $6\sqrt{25\ 4/5}$ =

   27._____

   A. 4 3/10
   C. 4 1/3
   B. 4 2/5
   D. none of the above

28. Change the following to decimal form $\frac{15}{14}$ 28._____

    A. .652   B. .655
    C. .625   D. none of the above

29. Take 1/6 of 372   29._____

    A. 57   B. 48
    C. 62   D. none of the above

30. Take 1/11 of 380.6   30._____

    A. 36.4   B. 34.6
    C. 36.6   D. none of the above

31. Find 7 1/2% of $3600   31._____

    A. $280   B. $270
    C. $275   D. none of the above

32. Find 16% of $215   32._____

    A. $34.40   B. $33.44
    C. $34.04   D. none of the above

33. Find 9 3/4% of 14   33._____

    A. 1.365   B. 1.356
    C. 1.565   D. none of the above

34. Find 3 4/5% of 15.5   34._____

    A. .597   B. .589
    C. .579   D. none of the above

35. Find 28% of $6535   35._____

    A. $1789.40   B. $1839.40
    C. $1788.49   D. none of the above

36. If .25 is divided by 40, the result is   36._____

    A. .00625   B. .0625
    C. .625   D. none of the above

37. The number 40 is 80% of   37._____

    A. 45   B. 50
    C. 55   D. none of the above

38. The number 24 is 60% of   38._____

    A. 30   B. 35
    C. 40   D. none of the above

39. If 9/10 of a number is 54, the number is   39._____

    A. 63   B. 60
    C. 74   D. none of the above

40. If 4/7 of a number is 64, the number is   40._____

    A.   122   B.   108
    C.   112   D.   none of the above

41. If 45 is divided by .15, the result is   41._____

    A.   30   B.   300
    C.   3000   D.   none of the above

42. If 29,021.251 is divided by 61.879, the result is   42._____

    A.   4690   B.   469
    C.   405   D.   none of the above

43. If 5,252.52 is divided by 62.53, the result is   43._____

    A.   84   B.   790
    C.   79   D.   none of the above

44. If 20% of a number is 62, the number is   44._____

    A.   295   B.   305
    C.   335   D.   none of the above

45. If 55% of a number is 220, the number is   45._____

    A.   405   B.   400
    C.   380   D.   none of the above

46. If the product of 160 multiplied by .06 is subtracted from the product of 17.5 multiplied by   46._____
.7, the result is

    A.   2.65   B.   3.2
    C.   4.1   D.   none of the above

47. Add the following lengths: 3 feet, 2 inches; 4 yards, 8 inches; 6 yards, 10 feet, 3 inches; 8   47._____
feet, 2 inches; and give the answer in feet and fractions thereof.

    A.   52 1/4'   B.   52 1/3'
    C.   53 1/4'   D.   None of the above

48. What is the net amount of a bill of $354 after a discount of 12% has been allowed?   48._____

    A. $311.25   B. $311.52
    C. $312.52   D.   None of the above

49. What is the net amount of a bill of $675.50 after a discount of 9% has been allowed?   49._____
(approximately)

    A. $641.07   B. $614.07
    C. $614.70   D.   None of the above

50. At 6 cents each, the cost of 215 plastic forks would be   50._____

    A. $15.06   B. $18.60
    C. $21.86   D.   none of the above

51. The sum of the numbers 46,385, 54,672, 6,210, 4,527, 38,925 is

    A. 150,917   B. 150,719
    C. 170,919   D. none of the above

51.____

52. The sum of the numbers 462, 75,832, 6,731, 60,235, 8,427 is

    A. 143,463   B. 151,687
    C. 174,823   D. none of the above

52.____

53. If a log measuring 8 feet, 4 inches is divided into five equal parts, each part is

    A. 1 foot   B. 1 foot, 1 3/4 inches
    C. 1 foot, 4 1/3 inches   D. none of the above

53.____

54. If erasers are sold at the rate of 5 for 18 cents, then 45 erasers will cost

    A. $1.62   B. $1.72
    C. $1.82   D. none of the above

54.____

55. If erasers are sold at the rate of 4 for 6 cents, then 120 erasers will cost

    A. $1.65   B. $1.75
    C. $1.85   D. none of the above

55.____

KEY (CORRECT ANSWERS)

1.	C	16.	D	31.	B	46.	A
2.	A	17.	A	32.	A	47.	A
3.	A	18.	B	33.	A	48.	B
4.	D	19.	B	34.	B	49.	C
5.	B	20.	B	35.	D	50.	D
6.	C	21.	A	36.	A	51.	B
7.	B	22.	D	37.	B	52.	B
8.	B	23.	C	38.	C	53.	D
9.	D	24.	A	39.	B	54.	A
10.	A	25.	D	40.	C	55.	D
11.	C	26.	C	41.	B		
12.	C	27.	A	42.	B		
13.	A	28.	C	43.	A		
14.	D	29.	C	44.	D		
15.	C	30.	B	45.	B		

SOLUTIONS TO PROBLEMS

1. (575)(269) = 154,675

2. (837)(720) = 602,640

3. (414)(961) = 397,854

4. (898)(303) = 272,094

5. (5623X2183) = 12,275,009

6. (913.67X1.04) = 950.2168

7. (313)(2.78) = 870.14

8. 69 + 23 + 12 + 14 = 118

9. 318 + 902 + 45 + 18 = 1283

10. $78.50 + .65 + $118.20 + $7.07 = 204.42

11. 8.6809 + .7516 + 1.5403 = 10.9728

12. 53 + 781 + 60 + 199 = 1093

13. 6 1/8 + 4 2/3 + 9 1/6 = 6 3/24 + 4 16/24 + 9 4/24 = 19 23/24

14. 2 1/2 + 8 1/4 + 7 1/6 = 2 6/12 + 8 3/12 + 7 2/12 = 17 11/12

15. $463.57 - $84.68 = $378.89

16. $1682.40 - $834.12 = $848.28

17. 991.17 - 916.18 = 74.99

18. 6241 - 861 = 5380

19. 8971.6 - 333.3 = 8638.3

20. 39 1/4 - 7 1/2 = 39 1/4 - 7 2/4 = 31 3/4

21. 5052 ÷ 6 = 842

22. 7596 ÷ 12 = 633

23. 368.501 ÷ 14 = 26.3215

24. $391 \cdot 73 \div 21 \approx 18 \cdot 654$

25. $175.5 \div 5.4 = 32.5$

26. $8\dfrac{3}{4} \div 2 = (\dfrac{67}{8})(\dfrac{1}{2}) = \dfrac{67}{16} = 4\dfrac{3}{16}$

27. $25\dfrac{4}{5} \div 6 = (\dfrac{129}{5})(\dfrac{1}{6}) = \dfrac{129}{30} = 4\dfrac{3}{10}$

28. $15/24 = .625$

29. $(1/6)(372) = 62$

30. $(1/11)(380.6) = 34.6$

31. $(.075)(\$3600) = \$270$

32. $(.16)(\$215) = \$34.40$

33. $9\dfrac{3}{4}\%$ of $14 = (\cdot 0975)(14) = 1 \cdot 365$

34. $3\ 4/5\%$ of $15.5 = (.038)(15.5) = .589$

35. $(.28)(\$6535) = \$1829.80$

36. $.25 \div 40 = .00625$

37. $40 = 80\%$ of $x \cdot$ Then, $x = 40 \div \cdot 80 = 50$

38. $24 = 60\%$ of x. Then, $x = 24 \div .60 = 40$

39. $9/10$ of $x = 54$. Then, $x = 54 \div 9/10 = 60$

40. $4/7$ of $x = 64$ Then, $x = 64 \div 4/7 = 112$

41. $45 \div .15 = 300$

42. $29,021.251 \div 61.879 = 469$

43. $5252.52 \div 62.53 = 84$

44. 20% of $x = 62$. Then, $x = 62 \div .20 = 310$

45. 55% of $x = 220$. Then, $x = 220 \div .55 = 400$

46. (17.5) (.7) - (160)(.06) = 12.25 - 9.6 = 2.65

47. 3 ft. 2 in. + 4 yds. 8 in. + 6 yds. 10 ft. 3 in. + 8 ft. 2 in. = 3 ft. 2 in. + 12 ft. 8 in. + 28 ft. 3 in. + 8 ft. 2 in. = 51 ft. 15 in. = 52 ft. 3 in. = 52 1/4 ft.

48. \$354 - (.12)(\$354) = \$354 - \$42.48 = \$311.52

49. \$675.50 - (.09)(\$675.50) ≈ \$675.50 - \$60.80 = \$614.70

50. (215)(.06) = \$12.90

51. 46,385 + 54,672 + 6210 + 4527 + 38,925 = 150,719

52. 462 + 75,832 + 6731 + 60,235 + 8427 = 151,687

53. 8 ft. 4 in. ÷ 5 = 100 in, ÷ 5 = 20 in. = 1 ft. 8 in.

54. Let x = cost. Then, 5/.18 = 45/x , 5x = 8.10, x = \$1.62

55. Let x = cost. Then, 4/.06 = 120/x , 4x = 7.20, x = \$1.80

ARITHMETICAL REASONING

EXAMINATION SECTION
TEST 1

DIRECTIONS: Each question or incomplete statement is followed by several suggested answers or completions. Select the one that BEST answers the question or completes the statement. *PRINT THE LETTER OF THE CORRECT ANSWER IN THE SPACE AT THE RIGHT.*

1. If it takes 2 men 9 days to do a job, how many men are needed to do the same job in 3 days?   1._____

   A. 4   B. 5   C. 6   D. 7

2. Suppose that a department operates 1,644 buildings. If one employee is needed for every 2 buildings, and one foreman is needed for every 18 employees, the number of foremen needed is CLOSEST to   2._____

   A. 45   B. 50   C. 55   D. 60

3. If 60 bars of soap cost the same as 2 gallons of wax, how many bars of soap can be bought for the price of 5 gallons of wax?   3._____

   A. 120   B. 150   C. 180   D. 300

4. An employee waxes 275 sq.ft. of floor on Monday, 352 sq.ft. on Tuesday, 179 sq.ft. on Wednesday, and 302 sq.ft. on Thursday.
   In order to average 280 sq.ft. of floor waxed a day, how many square feet of floor must he wax on Friday?   4._____

   A. 264   B. 278   C. 292   D. 358

5. A project covers 35 acres altogether. Lawns, playgrounds, and walks take up 28 acres and the rest is given over to buildings.
   What percentage of the total area is given over to buildings?   5._____

   A. 7%   B. 20%   C. 25%   D. 28%

6. When preparing for a mopping operation, fill the standard 16 quart bucket to the 3/4 full mark with warm water. Then add detergent at the rate of 2 oz. per gallon of water and disinfectant at the rate of 1 oz. to 3 gallons of water. According to these directions, the amount of detergent and disinfectant to add to 3/4 of a bucket of warm water is _____ oz. detergent and _____ oz. disinfectant.   6._____

   A. 4; 1/2   B. 5; 3/4   C. 6; 1   D. 8; 1 1/4

7. If corn brooms weigh 32 lbs. a dozen, the average weight of one corn broom is CLOS-EST to _____ lbs. _____ oz.   7._____

   A. 2; 14   B. 2; 11   C. 2; 9   D. 2; 6

8. At the beginning of the year, a foreman has 7 dozen electric bulbs in stock. During the year, he receives a shipment of 14 dozen bulbs, and also replaces 5 burned out bulbs a month in each of 3 buildings in his area. How many electric bulbs does he have on hand at the end of the year? _____dozen.   8.___

   A. 3   B. 6   C. 8   D. 12

9. A project has 4 buildings, each 14 floors high. Each floor has 10 apartments. If 35% of the apartments in the project have 3 rooms or less, how many apartments have 4 or more rooms?   9.___

   A. 196   B. 210   C. 364   D. 406

10. An employee takes 1 hour and 30 minutes a day to sweep 30 flights of stairs. How many flights of stairs does he sweep in a month if he spends a total of 30 hours doing this job and works at the same rate?   10.___

   A. 200   B. 300   C. 600   D. 900

11. During a month, Employee A washed 30 windows, Employee B washed 4 times as many windows as Employee A, and Employee C washed half as many windows as Employee B. The TOTAL number of windows washed by all three men together during this month is   11.___

   A. 180   B. 210   C. 240   D. 330

12. How much would it cost to completely fence in the playground area shown at the right with fencing costing $7.50 a foot?   12.___
    A. $615.00
    B. $820.00
    C. $885.00
    D. $960.00

13. A drill bit measures .625 inches. The fractional equivalent, in inches, is   13.___

    A. 9/16   B. 5/8   C. 11/16   D. 3/4

14. The number of cubic yards of sand required to fill a bin measuring 12 feet by 6 feet by 4 feet is MOST NEARLY   14.___

    A. 8   B. 11   C. 48   D. 96

15. Assume that you are assigned to put down floor tiles in a room measuring 8 feet by 10 feet. Individual tiles measure 9 inches by 9 inches. The total number of floor tiles required to cover the entire floor is MOST NEARLY   15.___

    A. 107   B. 121   C. 142   D. 160

16. Lumber is usually sold by the board foot, and a board foot is defined as a board one foot   16._____
square and one inch thick.
If the price of one board foot of lumber is 90 cents and you need 20 feet of lumber 6
inches wide and 1 inch thick, the cost of the 20 feet of lumber is

    A. $9.00   B. $12.00   C. $18.00   D. $24.00

17. For a certain plumbing repair job, you need three lengths of pipe, 12 1/4 inches, 6 1/2   17._____
inches, and 8 5/8 inches.
If you cut these three lengths from the same piece of pipe, which is 36 inches long,
and each cut consumes 1/8 inch of pipe, the length of pipe REMAINING after you have
cut out your three pieces should be _____ inches.

    A. 7 1/4   B. 7 7/8   C. 8 1/4   D. 8 7/8

18. A maintenance bond for a roadway pavement is in an amount of 10% of the estimated   18._____
cost.
If the estimated cost is $8,000,000, the maintenance bond is

    A. $8,000   B. $80,000   C. $800,000   D. $8,000,000

19. Specifications require that a core be taken every 700 square yards of paved roadway or   19._____
fraction thereof. A 100 foot by 200 foot rectangular area would require _____ core(s).

    A. 1   B. 2   C. 3   D. 4

20. An applicant must file a map at a scale of 1" = 40'. Six inches on the map represents   20._____
_____ feet on the ground.

    A. 600   B. 240   C. 120   D. 60

21. A 100' x 110' lot has an area of MOST NEARLY _____ acre.   21._____

    A. 1/8   B. 1/4   C. 3/8   D. 1/2

22. 1 inch is MOST NEARLY equal to _____ feet.   22._____

    A. .02   B. .04   C. .06   D. .08

23. The area of the triangle EFG shown   23._____
at the right is MOST NEARLY _____ sq. ft.

    A. 36   B. 42   C. 48   D. 54

24. Specifications state: As further security for the faithful performance of this contract, the   24._____
Comptroller shall deduct, and retain until the final payment, 10% of the value of the work
certified for payment in each partial payment voucher, until the amount so deducted and
retained shall equal 5% of the contract price or in the case of a unit price contract, 5% of
the estimated amount to be paid to the Contractor under the contract.
For a $300,000 contract, the amount to be retained at the end of the contract is

    A. $5,000   B. $10,000   C. $15,000   D. $20,000

25. Asphalt was laid for a length of 210 feet on the entire width of a street whose curb-to-curb   25._____
distance is 30 feet. The number of square yards covered with asphalt is MOST NEARLY

    A. 210   B. 700   C. 2,100   D. 6,300

KEY (CORRECT ANSWERS)

1.	C		11.	B
2.	A		12.	C
3.	B		13.	B
4.	C		14.	B
5.	B		15.	C
6.	C		16.	A
7.	B		17.	C
8.	B		18.	C
9.	C		19.	D
10.	C		20.	B

21.	B
22.	D
23.	A
24.	C
25.	B

———

SOLUTIONS TO PROBLEMS

1. (2)(9) = 18 man-days. Then, 18 ÷ 3 = 6 men

2. The number of employees = 1644 ÷ 2 = 822. The number of foremen needed
    = 822 ÷ 18 ≈ 45

3. 1 gallon of wax costs the same as 60 ÷ 2 = 30 bars of soap. Thus, 5 gallons of wax costs
    the same as (5)(30) = 150 bars of soap.

4. To average 280 sq.ft. for five days means a total of (5)(280) = 1400 sq.ft. for all five days.
    The number of square feet to be waxed on Friday = 1400 - (275+352+179+302) = 292

5. The acreage for buildings is 35 - 28 = 7. Then, 7/35 = 20%

6. (16)(3/4) = 12 quarts = 3 gallons. The amount of detergent, in ounces, is (2)(3) = 6. The
    amount of disinfectant is 1 oz.

7. One corn broom weighs 32 ÷ 12 = 2 2/3 lbs. ≈ 2 lbs. 11 oz.

8. Number of bulbs at the beginning of the year = (7)(12) + (14)(12) = 252. Number of bulbs
    replaced over an entire year = (5)(3)(12) = 180. The number of unused bulbs = 252 - 180
    = 72 = 6 dozen.

9. Total number of apartments = (4)(14)(10) = 560. The number of apartments with at least
    4 rooms = (.65)(560) = 364.

10. 30 ÷ 1 1/2 = 20. Then, (20)(30) = 600 flights of stairs

11. The number of windows washed by A, B, C were 30, 120, and 60. Their total is 210.

12. The two missing dimensions are 26 - 14 = 12 ft. and 33 - 9 = 24 ft. Perimeter = 9 + 12 +
    33 + 26 + 24 + 14 = 118 ft. Thus, total cost of fencing = (118)($7.50) = $885.00

13. $.625 = \dfrac{625}{1000} = \dfrac{5}{8}$

14. (12)(6)(4) = 288 cu.ft. Now, 1 cu.yd. = 27 cu.ft.; 288 cu.ft. is equivalent to 10 2/3 or about
    11 cu.yds.

15. 144 sq.in. = 1 sq.ft. The room measures (8 ft.)x(10 ft.) = 80 sq.ft. = 11,520 sq.in. Each tile
    measures (9)(9) = 81 sq.in. The number of tiles needed = 11,520 ÷ 81 = 142.2 or about
    142.

16. 20 ft. by 6 in. = (20 ft.)(1/2 ft.) = 10 sq.ft. Then, (10X.90) = $9.00

17. There will be 3 cuts in making 3 lengths of pipe, and these 3 cuts will use (3)(1/8) = 3/8
    in. of pipe. The amount of pipe remaining after the 3 pieces are removed = 36 - 12 1/4
    - 6 1/2 - 8 5/8 - 3/8 = 8 1/4 in.

18. The maintenance bond = (.10)($8,000,000) = $800,000

19. (100)(200) = 20,000 sq.ft. = 20,000 ÷ 9 ≈ 2222 sq.yds. Then, 2222 ÷ 700 ≈ 3.17. Since a core must be taken for each 700 sq.yds. plus any left over fraction, 4 cores will be needed.

20. Six inches means (6)(40) = 240 ft. of actual length.

21. (100 ft.)(110 ft.) = 11,000 sq.ft. ≈ 1222 sq.yds. Then, since 1 acre = 4840 sq.yds., 1222 sq.yds. is equivalent to about 1/4 acre.

22. 1 in. = 1/12 ft. ≈ .08 ft.

23. Area of $\triangle$ EFG = (1/2)(8)(6) + (1/2)(4)(6) = 36 sq.ft.

24. The amount to be retained = (.05)($300,000) = $15,000

25. (210)(30) = 6300 sq.ft. Since 1 sq.yd. = 9 sq.ft., 6300 sq.ft. equals 700 sq.yds.

TEST 2

DIRECTIONS: Each question or incomplete statement is followed by several suggested answers or completions. Select the one that BEST answers the question or completes the statement. *PRINT THE LETTER OF THE CORRECT ANSWER IN THE SPACE AT THE RIGHT.*

1. The TOTAL length of four pieces of 2" pipe, whose lengths are 7'3 1/2", 4'2 3/16", 5'7 5/16", and 8'5 7/8", respectively, is

   A. 24'6 3/4"   B. 24'7 15/16"
   C. 25'5 13/16"   D. 25'6 7/8"

   1._____

2. Under the same conditions, the group of pipes that gives the SAME flow as one 6" pipe is (neglecting friction) _____ pipes.

   A. 3 3"   B. 4 3"   C. 2 4"   D. 3 4"

   2._____

3. A water storage tank measures 5' long, 4' wide, and 6' deep and is filled to the 5 1/2' mark with water.
   If one cubic foot of water weighs 62 pounds, the number of pounds of water required to COMPLETELY fill the tank is

   A. 7,440   B. 6,200   C. 1,240   D. 620

   3._____

4. A hot water line made of copper has a straight horizontal run of 150 feet and, when installed, is at a temperature of 45°F. In use, its temperature rises to 190°F.
   If the coefficient of expansion for copper is 0.0000095" per foot per degree F, the total expansion, in inches, in the run of pipe is given by the product of 150 multiplied by 0.0000095 by

   A. 145   B. 145 x 12
   C. 145 divided by 12 D. 145 x 12 x 12

   4._____

5. To dig a trench 3'0" wide, 50'0" long, and 5'6" deep, the total number of cubic yards of earth to be removed is MOST NEARLY

   A. 30   B. 90   C. 140   D. 825

   5._____

6. If it costs $65 for 20 feet of subway rail, the cost of 150 feet of this rail will be

   A. $487.50   B. $512.00   C. $589.50   D. $650.00

   6._____

7. The number of cubic feet of concrete it takes to fill a form 10 feet long, 3 feet wide, and 6 inches deep is

   A. 12   B. 15   C. 20   D. 180

   7._____

8. The sum of 4 1/16, 51/4, 3 5/8, and 4 7/16 is

   A. 17 3/16   B. 17 1/4   C. 17 5/16   D. 17 3/8

   8._____

9. If you earn $10.20 per hour and time and one-half for working over 40 hours, your gross salary for a week in which you worked 42 hours would be

   A. $408.00   B. $428.40   C. $438.60   D. $770.80

   9._____

10. A drill bit, used to drill holes in track ties, has a diameter of 0.75 inches.   10.___
When expressed as a fraction, the diameter of this drill bit is

    A. 1/4"   B. 3/8"   C. 1/2"   D. 3/4"

11. Three dozen shovels were purchased for use.   11.___
If the shovels were used at the rate of nine a week, the number of weeks that the three
dozen lasted was

    A. 3   B. 4   C. 9   D. 12

12. Assume that you earn $20,000 per year.   12.___
If twenty percent of your pay is deducted for taxes, social security, and pension, your
weekly take-home pay will be MOST NEARLY

    A. $280   B. $308   C. $328   D. $344

13. If a measurement scaled from a drawing is one inch, and the scale of the drawing is 1/8   13.___
inch to the foot, then the one inch measurement would represent an ACTUAL length of

    A. 8 feet   B. 2 feet
    C. 1/8 of a foot   D. 8 inches

14. Tiles 12" x 12" are used to lay a floor having the dimensions 10'0" x 12'0".   14.___
The MINIMUM number of tiles needed to completely cover the floor is

    A. 60   B. 96   C. 120   D. 144

15. The volume of concrete in a strip of sidewalk 30 feet long by 4 feet wide by 3 inches thick   15.___
is _____ cubic feet.

    A. 30   B. 120   C. 240   D. 360

16. To change a quantity of cubic feet into an equivalent quantity of cubic yards, _____ the   16.___
quantity by _____.

    A. multiply; 9   B. divide; 9
    C. multiply; 27   D. divide; 27

17. If a pump can deliver 50 gallons of water per minute, then the time needed for this pump   17.___
to empty an excavation containing 5,800 gallons of water is _____ hour(s) _____ minutes.

    A. 2; 12   B. 1; 56   C. 1; 44   D. 1; 32

18. The sum of 3 1/6", 4 1/4", 3 5/8", and 5 7/16" is   18.___

    A. 15 9/16"   B. 16 1/8"   C. 16 23/48"   D. 16 3/4"

19. If a measurement scaled from a drawing is 2 inches, and the scale of the drawing is 1/8   19.___
inch to the foot, then the two inch measurement would represent an ACTUAL length of

    A. 8 feet   B. 4 feet
    C. 1/4 of a foot   D. 16 feet

20. A room is 7'6" wide by 9'0" long with a ceiling height of 8'0". One gallon of flat paint will cover approximately 400 square feet of wall.
The number of gallons of this paint required to paint the walls of this room, making no deductions for windows or doors, is MOST NEARLY

   20._____

   A. 1/4   B. 1/2   C. 2/3   D. 1

21. The cost of a certain job is broken down as follows:

   21._____

Materials	$3,750
Rental of equipment	1,200
Labor	3,150

   The percentage of the total cost of the job that can be charged to materials is MOST NEARLY

   A. 40%   B. 42%   C. 44%   D. 46%

22. By trial, it is found that by using two cubic feet of sand, a 5 cubic foot batch of concrete is produced. Using the same proportions, the amount of sand required to produce 2 cubic yards of concrete is MOST NEARLY _____ cubic feet.

   22._____

   A. 20   B. 22   C. 24   D. 26

23. It takes 4 men 6 days to do a certain job.
Working at the same speed, the number of days it will take 3 men to do this job is

   23._____

   A. 7   B. 8   C. 9   D. 10

24. The cost of rawl plugs is $27.50 per gross. The cost of 2,448 rawl plugs is

   24._____

   A. $467.50   B. $472.50   C. $477.50   D. $482.50

25. In a certain district, the area of a building may be no longer than 55% of the area of the lot on which it stands. On a rectangular lot 75 ft. by 125 ft., the maximum permissible area of building is, in square feet, MOST NEARLY

   25._____

   A. 5,148   B. 5,152   C. 5,156   D. 5,160

KEY (CORRECT ANSWERS)

1.	D		11.	B
2.	B		12.	B
3.	D		13.	A
4.	A		14.	C
5.	A		15.	A
6.	A		16.	D
7.	B		17.	B
8.	D		18.	C
9.	C		19.	D
10.	D		20.	C

21.	D
22.	B
23.	B
24.	A
25.	C

––––––––

SOLUTIONS TO PROBLEMS

1. $3\frac{1}{6}" + 4\frac{1}{4}" + 3\frac{5}{8}" + 5\frac{7}{16}" + -3\frac{8}{48}" + 4\frac{12}{48}" + 3\frac{30}{48}" + 5\frac{21}{48}" = 15\frac{71}{48}" = 16\frac{23}{48}"$

2. The flow of a 6" pipe is measured by the cross-sectional area. Since diameter = 6", radius = 3", and so area = 9π sq.in. A single 3" pipe would have a cross-sectional area of $(3/2)\pi$ sq.in. = 2.25π sq.in. Now, $9 \div / 2.25 = 4$. Thus, four 3" pipes is equivalent, in flow, to one 6" pipe.

3. (5x4x6) - (5x4x5 1/2) = 10. Then, (10)(62) = 620 pounds.

4. The total expansion = (150')(.0000095"/1 ft.)(190°-45°). So, the last factor is 145.

5. (3')(50')(5 1/2') = 825 cu.ft. Since 1 cu.yd. = 27 cu.ft., 825 cu.ft. cu.yds.

6. $150 \div 20 = 7.5$. Then, (7.5)($65) = $487.50

7. (10')(3')(1/2') = 15 cu.ft.

8. $4\frac{1}{16} + 5\frac{4}{16} + 3\frac{10}{16} + 4\frac{7}{16} = 16\frac{22}{16} = 17\frac{3}{8}$

9. Gross salary = ($10.20)(40) + ($15.30)(2) = $438.60

10. $75" = \frac{75}{100}" = \frac{3}{4}"$

11. 3 dozen = 36 shovels. Then, $36 \div 9 = 4$ weeks

12. Since 20% is deducted, the take-home pay = ($20,000)(.80) = $16,000 for the year, which is $16,000 \div 52 \approx $308 per week.

13. A scale drawing where 1/8" means an actual size of 1 ft. implies that a scale drawing of 1" means an actual size of (1')(8) = 8'

14. (10')(12') = 120 sq.ft. Since each tile is 1 sq.ft., a total of 120 tiles will be used.

15. (30')(4')(1/4') = 30 cu.ft.

16. To convert a given number of cubic feet into an equivalent number of cubic yards, divide by 27.

17. $5800 \div 50 = 116$ min. = 1 hour 56 minutes

18. $3\frac{1}{6}" + 4\frac{1}{4}" + 3\frac{5}{8}" + 5\frac{7}{16}" + = 3\frac{8}{48}" + 4\frac{12}{48}" + 3\frac{30}{48}" + 5\frac{21}{48}" = 15\frac{71}{48}" = 16\frac{23}{48}"$

19. $2 \div 1/8 = 16$, so a 2" drawing represents an actual length of 16 feet.

20. The area of the 4 walls = 2(7 1/2')(8') + 2(9')(8') = 264 sq.ft. Then, 264 ÷ 400 = .66 or about 2/3 gallon of paint.

21. $3750 + $1200 + $3150 = $8100. Then, $3750/$8100 ≈ 46%

22. 2 cu.yds. ÷ 5 cu.ft. = 54 ÷ 5 = 10.8. Now, (10.8)(2 cu.ft.) ≈ 22 cu.ft. Note: 2 cu.yds. = 54 cu.ft.

23. (4)(6) = 24 man-days. Then, 24 ÷ 3 = 8 days

24. 2448 ÷ 144 = 17. Then, (17)($27.50) = $467.50

25. (75')(125') = 9375 sq.ft. The maximum area of the building = (.55)(9375 sq.ft.) ≈ 5156 sq.ft.

TEST 3

DIRECTIONS: Each question or incomplete statement is followed by several suggested answers or completions. Select the one that BEST answers the question or completes the statement. *PRINT THE LETTER OF THE CORRECT ANSWER IN THE SPACE AT THE RIGHT.*

1. A steak weighed 2 pounds, 4 ounces. How much did it cost at $4.60 per pound?

   A. $7.80   B. $8.75   C. $9.90   D. $10.35

1.____

2. twenty pints of water just fill a pail. the capacity of the pail, in gallons, is

   A. 2   B. 2 1/4   C. 2 1/2   D. 2 3/4

2.____

3. The sum of 5/12 and 1/4 is

   A. 7/12   B. 2/3   C. 3/4   D. 5/6

3.____

4. The volume of earth, in cubic yards, excavated from a trench 4'0" wide by 5'6" deep by 18'6" long is MOST NEARLY

   A. 14.7   B. 15.1   C. 15.5   D. 15.9

4.____

5. 5/8 written as a decimal is

   A. 62.5   B. 6.25   C. .625   D. .0625

5.____

6. The number of cubic feet in a cubic yard is

   A. 9   B. 12   C. 27   D. 36

6.____

7. If it costs $16.20 to lay one square yard of asphalt, to lay a patch 15' by 15', it will cost MOST NEARLY

   A. $405.00   B. $3,645.00   C. $134.50   D. $243.00

7.____

8. You are assigned thirty (30) asphalt workers to be divided into two crews so that one crew will have 2/3 as many men as the other. The number of men you would put into the SMALLER crew is

   A. 10   B. 12   C. 14   D. 20

8.____

9. It takes 12 asphalt workers, working 6 hours a day, 5 days to complete a certain job. The number of days it will take 10 men, working 8 hours a day, to do the same job, assuming all work at the same rate, is

   A. 2 1/2   B. 3   C. 4 1/2   D. 6

9.____

10. A street is laid to a 3% grade. This means that in 150 ft., the street grade will rise

   A. 4 1/2 inches   B. 45 inches
   C. 4 1/2 feet   D. 45 feet

10.____

11. The sum of the following dimensions, 3 4/8, 4 1/8, 5 1/8, and 6 1/4, is   11._____

    A. 19   B. 19 1/8   C. 19 1/4   D. 19 1/2

12. A worker is paid $9.30 per hour.   12._____
If he works 8 hours each day on Monday, Tuesday, and Wednesday, 3 1/2 hours on
Thursday, and 3 hours on Friday, the TOTAL amount due him is

    A. $283.65   B. $289.15   C. $276.20   D. $285.35

13. The price of metal lath is $395.00 per 100 square yards. The cost of 527 square yards of   13._____
this lath is MOST NEARLY

    A. $2,076.50   B. $2,079.10   C. $2,081.70   D. $2,084.30

14. The total cost of applying 221 square yards of plaster board is $3,430.   14._____
The cost per square yard is MOST NEARLY

    A. $14.00   B. $14.50   C. $15.00   D. $15.50

15. In a three-coat plaster job, the scratch coat is 1/8 in. thick in front of the lath, the brown   15._____
coat is 3/16 in. thick, and the finish coat is 1/8 in. thick.
The TOTAL thickness of this plaster job, measured from the face of the lath, is

    A. 7/16"   B. 1/2"   C. 9/16"   D. 5/8"

16. If an asphalt worker earns $38,070 per year, his wages per month are MOST NEARLY   16._____

    A. $380.70   B. $735.00   C. $3,170.00   D. $3,807.00

17. The sum of 4 1/2 inches, 3 1/4 inches, and 7 1/2 inches is 1 foot _____ inches.   17._____

    A. 3   B. 3 1/4   C. 3 1/2   D. 4

18. The area of a rectangular asphalt patch, 9 ft. 3 in. by 6 ft. 9 in., is _____ square feet.   18._____

    A. 54   B. 54 1/4   C. 54 1/2   D. 62 7/16

19. The number of cubic feet in a cubic yard is   19._____

    A. 3   B. 9   C. 16   D. 27

20. A 450 ft. long street with a grade of 2% will have one end of the street higher than the   20._____
other end by _____ feet.

    A. 2   B. 44   C. 9   D. 20

21. If the drive wheel of a roller is 6 ft. in diameter and the tiller wheel is 4 ft. in diameter,   21._____
whenever the drive wheel makes a complete revolution on a straight pass, the tiller wheel
makes _____ revolution(s).

    A. 1   B. 1 1/4   C. 1 1/2   D. 2

22. A point on the centerline of a street is marked: Station 42 + 51. Another point on the cen-   22._____
terline 30 feet from the first is marked Station 42+81.
A third should be marked Station

    A. 12+51   B. 42+21   C. 45+51   D. 72+51

23. In twenty minutes, a truck moving with a speed of 30 miles an hour will cover a distance of _____ miles.   23._____

    A. 3   B. 5   C. 10   D. 30

24. The number of pounds in a ton is   24._____

    A. 500   B. 1,000   C. 2,000   D. 5,000

25. During his summer vacation, a boy earned $45.00 per day and saved 60% of his earnings.   25._____
If he worked 45 days, how much did he save during his vacation?

    A. $15.00   B. $18.00   C. $1,215.00   D. $22.50

KEY (CORRECT ANSWERS)

1. D	11. A
2. C	12. A
3. B	13. C
4. B	14. D
5. C	15. A
6. C	16. C
7. A	17. B
8. B	18. D
9. C	19. D
10. C	20. C

21. C
22. B
23. C
24. C
25. C

SOLUTIONS TO PROBLEMS

1. ($4.60)(2 1/4 lbs.) = $10.35

2. 1 gallon = 8 pints, so 20 pints = 20/8 = 2 1/2 gallons

3. $\dfrac{5}{12}+\dfrac{1}{4}=\dfrac{5}{12}+\dfrac{3}{12}=\dfrac{8}{12}=\dfrac{2}{3}$

4. (4')(5 1/2')(18 1/2') = 407 cu.ft. Since 1 cu.yd. = 27 cu.ft., 407 cu.ft. $\approx$ 15.1 cu.yds.

5. 5/8=5 $\div$ 8.000 = .625

6. There are (3)(3)(3) =27 cu.ft. in a cu.yd.

7. (15')(15') = 225 sq.ft. = 25 sq.yds. Then, ($16.20)(25) = $405.00

8. Let 2x = size of smaller crew and 3x = size of larger crew. Then, 2x + 3x = 30. Solving, x = 6. Thus, the smaller crew consists of 12 workers.

9. (12)(6)(5) = 360 worker-days. Then, 360 $\div$ [(10)(8)] = 4 1/2 days

10. (.03)(150') = 4 1/2 ft.

11. $3\dfrac{4}{8}+4\dfrac{1}{8}+5\dfrac{1}{8}+6\dfrac{2}{8}=18\dfrac{8}{8}=19$

12. ($9.30)(8+8+8+3 1/2+3) = ($9.30)(30 1/2) = $283.65

13. The cost of 527 sq.yds. = (5.27)($395.00) = $2081.65 $\approx$ $2081.70

14. $3430 $\div$ 221 $\approx$ $15.50

15. $\dfrac{1}{8}"+\dfrac{3}{16}"+\dfrac{1}{8}"=\dfrac{2}{16}"+\dfrac{3}{16}"+\dfrac{2}{16}"=\dfrac{7}{16}"$

16. $38,070 $\div$ 12 = $3172.50 $\approx$ $3170.00 per month

17. 4 1/2" + 3 1/4" + 7 1/2" = 15 1/4" = 1 ft. 3 1/4 in.

18. 9 ft. 3 in. = 9 1/4 ft., 6 ft. 9 in. = 6 3/4 ft. Area = (9 1/4) (6 3/4) – 62 7/16 sq.ft.

19. A cubic yard = (3)(3)(3) = 27 cubic feet

20. (450')(.02) = 9 ft.

21. 6/4 = 1 1/2 revolutions

22. Station 42 + 51
    30 ft away would be 51 + 30 = 81 OR 51 - 30 = 21
    Station 42 + 81 or 42 + 21 (ANSWER: B)

23. 30 miles in 60 minutes means 10 miles in 20 minutes.

24. There are 2000 pounds in a ton.

25. ($45.00)(.60) = $27.00 savings per day. For 45 days, his savings is (45)($27.00) = $1215.00

———————

ARITHMETICAL REASONING
EXAMINATION SECTION
TEST 1

DIRECTIONS: Each question or incomplete statement is followed by several suggested answers or completions. Select the one that BEST answers the question or completes the statement. *PRINT THE LETTER OF THE CORRECT ANSWER IN THE SPACE AT THE RIGHT.*

1. A supplier quotes a list price of $172.00 less 15 and 10 percent for twelve tools. The actual cost for these twelve tools is MOST NEARLY

   A. $146　　　B. $132　　　C. $129　　　D. $112

   1.＿＿＿

2. If the diameter of a circular piece of sheet metal is 1 1/2 feet, the area, in square inches, is MOST NEARLY

   A. 1.77　　　B. 2.36　　　C. 254　　　D. 324

   2.＿＿＿

3. The sum of 5'6", 7'3", 9'3 1/2", and 3'7 1/4" is

   A. 19'8 1/2"　　　B. 22' 1/2"　　　C. 25'7 3/4"　　　D. 28'8 3/4"

   3.＿＿＿

4. If the floor area of one shop is 15' by 21'3" and the size of an adjacent shop is 18' by 30'6", then the TOTAL floor area of these two shops is ＿＿＿ square feet.

   A. 1127.75　　　B. 867.75　　　C. 549.0　　　D. 318.75

   4.＿＿＿

5. The fraction which is equal to 0.875 is

   A. 7/16　　　B. 5/8　　　C. 3/4　　　D. 7/8

   5.＿＿＿

6. The sum of 1/2, 2 1/32, 4 3/16, and 1 7/8 is MOST NEARLY

   A. 9.593　　　B. 9.625　　　C. 9.687　　　D. 10.593

   6.＿＿＿

7. If the base of a right triangle is 9" and the altitude is 12", the length of the third side will be

   A. 13"　　　B. 14"　　　C. 15"　　　D. 16"

   7.＿＿＿

8. If a steel bar 1" in diameter and 12' long weighs 32 lbs., then the weight of a piece of this bar 5'9" long is MOST NEARLY ＿＿＿ lbs.

   A. 15.33　　　B. 15.26　　　C. 16.33　　　D. 15.06

   8.＿＿＿

9. The diameter of a circle whose circumference is 12" is MOST NEARLY

   A. 3.82"　　　B. 3.72"　　　C. 3.62"　　　D. 3.52"

   9.＿＿＿

10. A dimension of 39/64 inches converted to decimals is MOST NEARLY

    A. .600"　　　B. .609"　　　C. .607"　　　D. .611"

    10.＿＿＿

11. A farm worker was paid a weekly wage of $415.20 for a 44-hour work week. As a result   11.____
of a new labor contract, he is paid $431.40 a week for a 40-hour work week with time and
one-half pay for time worked in excess of 40 hours in any work week.
If he continues to work 44 hours weekly under the new contract, the amount by which
his average hourly rate for a 44-hour work week under the new contract exceeds the
hourly rate previously paid him lies between _____ and _____, inclusive.

    A. 80¢; $1.00   B. $1.00; $1.20
    C. $1.25; $1.45   D. $1.50; $1.70

12. The sum of 4 feet 3 1/4 inches, 7 feet 2 1/2 inches, and 11 feet 1/4 inch is _____ feet   12.____
_____ inches.

    A. 21; 6 1/4   B. 22; 6   C. 23; 5   D. 24; 5 3/4

13. The number 0.038 is read as   13.____

    A. 38 tenths   B. 38 hundredths
    C. 38 thousandths   D. 38 ten-thousandths

14. Assume that an employee is paid at the rate of $5.43 per hour with time and a half for   14.____
overtime past 40 hours in a week.
If he works 43 hours in a week, his gross weekly pay is

    A. $217.20   B. $219.20   C. $229.59   D. $241.64

15. The sum of the following dimensions: 3'2 1/4", 8 7/8", 2'6 3/8", 2'9 3/4", and 1'0" is   15.____

    A. 16'7 1/4"   B. 10'7 1/4"   C. 10'3 1/4"   D. 9'3 1/4"

16. Two gears are meshed together and have a gear ratio of 6 to 1.   16.____
If the small gear rotates 120 revolutions per minute, the large gear rotates at

    A. 20   B. 40   C. 60   D. 720

17. The vacuum side of a compound gage reads 14 inches of vacuum. The barometer read-   17.____
ing is 29.76 inches of mercury. The equivalent absolute pressure of the compound gage
reading, in inches of mercury, is MOST likely

    A. 15.06   B. 15.76   C. 43.06   D. 43.76

18. The fraction 5/8 expressed as a decimal is   18.____

    A. 0.125   B. 0.412   C. 0.625   D. 0.875

19. If 300 feet of a certain size pipe weighs 450 pounds, the number of pounds that 100 feet   19.____
will weigh is

    A. 1,350   B. 150   C. 300   D. 250

20. As an oiler, you work for a facility that has automobiles that use, on the average, 600   20.____
quarts of one grade of lubricating oil every month.
The number of one-gallon cans of the above oil that should be ordered each month to
meet this requirement is

    A. 100   B. 125   C. 140   D. 150

21. The inside dimensions of a rectangular oil gravity tank are: height 15", width 9", length 10".   21._____
The amount of oil in the tank, in gallons, (231 cu.in. = 1 gallon), when the oil level is 9" high, is MOST NEARLY

  A. 2.3   B. 3.5   C. 5.2   D. 5.8

22. If 30 gallons of oil cost $76.80, 45 gallons of oil at the same rate will cost   22._____

  A. $91.20   B. $115.20   C. $123.20   D. $131.20

23. If an oiler earns $18,000 in the first six months of a year and receives a 10% raise in salary for the next six months of the same year, his TOTAL earnings for the year will be   23._____

  A. $36,000   B. $37,500   C. $37,800   D. $39,600

24. If the cost of lubricating oil increases 15%, then a gallon of oil which used to cost $10.00 will now cost MOST NEARLY   24._____

  A. $10.50   B. $11.00   C. $11.50   D. $12.00

25. The sum of 7/8", 3/4", 1/2", and 3/8" is   25._____

  A. 2 1/8"   B. 2 1/4"   C. 2 3/8"   D. 2 1/2"

KEY (CORRECT ANSWERS)

1. B		11. A		
2. C		12. B		
3. C		13. C		
4. B		14. D		
5. D		15. C		
6. A		16. A		
7. C		17. B		
8. A		18. C		
9. A		19. B		
10. B		20. D		

21. B
22. B
23. C
24. C
25. D

SOLUTIONS TO PROBLEMS

1. Actual cost = ($172)(,85)(.90) = $131.58 $\approx$ $132

2. Radius = .75', then area = (3.14)(.75)^2 $\approx$ 1.77 sq.ft.
   Since 1 sq.ft. = 144 sq.in., the area $\approx$ 254 sq.in.

3. 5'6" + 7'3" + 9'3 1/2" + 3'7 1/4" = 24'19 3/4" = 25'7 3/4"

4. Total area = (15)(21.25) + (18)(30.5) = 867.75 sq.ft.

5. .875 = 875/1000 =7/8

6. 1 1/2 + 2 1/32 +4 3/16 +1 7/8 = 8 51/32 = 9 19/32 = 9.593

7. Third side = $\sqrt{9^2+12^2}$ = $\sqrt{225}$ =15"

8. Let x = weight. Then, 12/32 = 5.75/x . Solving, x $\approx$ 15.33 lbs.

9. 12" = (3.14)(diameter), so diameter $\approx$ 3.82"

10. $\frac{39}{64}$" =.609375" $\approx$ .609"

11. Under his new contract, the weekly wage for 44 hours can be found by first determining his hourly rate for the first 40 hours = $431.40 $\div$ 40 $\approx$ $10.80. Now, his time and one-half pay will =($10.80)(1.5) = $16.20. His weekly wage for the new contract = $431.40 + (4)($16.20) = $496,20. His new hourly rate for 44 hours = $496.20 $\div$ 44 $\approx$ $10.34. Under the old contract, his hourly rate for 44 hours was $415.20 $\div$ 44 = $9.44. His hourly rate increase = $10.34 - $9.44 = $0.90. (Answer key: between $0.80 and $1.00)

12. 4'3 1/4" + 7'2 1/2" + 11' 1/4" = 22'6"

13. .038 = 38 thousandths

14. ($5.43)(40) + ($8.145)(3) = $241.64

15. 3'2 1/4" + 8 7/8" + 2'6 3/8" + 2'9 3/4" + 1'0" = 8'25 18/8" = 10'3 1/4"

16. The gear ratio is inversely proportional to the gear size. Let x = large gear's rpm. Then, 6/1 = 120/x . Solving, x = 20

17. Subtract 14 from 29.76

18. 5/8 = .625

19. Let x = number of pounds. Then, 300/450 = 100/x . Solving, x = 150

20. 600 quarts = 150 gallons, since 4 quarts = 1 gallon

21. (9")(9")(10") = 810 cu.in. Then, 810 $\div$ 231 $\approx$ 3.5

22. Let x = unknown cost. Then, 30/$76.00 = 45/x. Solving, x = $115.20

23. $18,000 + ($18,000)(1.10) = $37,800

24. ($10.00)(1.15) = $11.50

25. 7/8" + 3/4" + 1/2" + 3/8" = 20/8" = 2 1/2"

TEST 2

DIRECTIONS: Each question or incomplete statement is followed by several suggested answers or completions. Select the one that BEST answers the question or completes the statement. *PRINT THE LETTER OF THE CORRECT ANSWER IN THE SPACE AT THE RIGHT.*

1. A sheet metal plate has been cut in the form of a right triangle with sides of 5, 12, and 13 inches.
   The area of this plate, in square inches, is

   A. 30   B. 32 1/2   C. 60   D. 78

   1.____

2. If steel weighs 480 lbs. per cubic foot, the weight of an 18" x 18" x 2" steel base plate is _____ lbs.

   A. 180   B. 216   C. 427   D. 648

   2.____

3. By trial, it is found that by using 2 cubic feet of sand, a 5 cubic foot batch of concrete is produced.
   Using the same proportions, the amount of sand, in cubic feet, required to produce 2 cubic yards of concrete is MOST NEARLY

   A. 7   B. 22   C. 27   D. 45

   3.____

4. The total number of cubic yards of earth to be removed to make a trench 3'9" wide, 25'0" long, and 4'3" deep is MOST NEARLY

   A. 53.1   B. 35.4   C. 26.6   D. 14.8

   4.____

5. A large number of 2 x 4 studs, some 10'5" long and some 6'5 1/2" long, are required for a job.
   To minimize waste, it would be PREFERABLE to order lengths of _____ feet.

   A. 16   B. 17   C. 18   D. 19

   5.____

6. A 6" pipe is connected to a 4" pipe through a reducer. If 100 cubic feet of water is flowing through the 6" pipe per minute, the flow, in cubic feet, per minute through the 4" pipe is

   A. 225   B. 100   C. 66.6   D. 44.4

   6.____

7. If steel weighs 0.28 pounds per cubic inch, then the weight, in pounds, of a 2" square steel bar 120" long is MOST NEARLY

   A. 115   B. 125   C. 135   D. 155

   7.____

8. A three-inch diameter steel bar two feet long weighs MOST NEARLY (assume steel weighs 480 lbs./cu.ft.) _____ lbs.

   A. 48   B. 58   C. 68   D. 78

   8.____

9. The area of a circular plate will be reduced by 5% if a sector removed from it has an angle of _____ degrees.

   A. 18   B. 24   C. 32   D. 60

   9.____

10. If a 4 1/16 inch shaft wears six thousandths of an inch, the NEW diameter will be _____ inches.

    A. 4.0031   B. 4.0565   C. 4.0578   D. 4.0605

10.____

11. A set of mechanical plan drawings is drawn to a scale of 1/8" = 1 foot. If a length of pipe measures 15 7/16" on the drawing, the ACTUAL length of the pipe is _____ feet.

    A. 121.5   B. 122.5   C. 123.5   D. 124.5

11.____

12. An electrical drawing is drawn to a scale of 1/4" = 1'. If a length of conduit on the drawing measures 7 3/8", the actual length of the conduit, in feet, is

    A. 7.5   B. 15.5   C. 22.5   D. 29.5

12.____

13. Assume that you have assigned 6 mechanics to do a job that must be finished in 4 days. At the end of 3 days, your men have completed only two-thirds of the job. In order to complete the job on time and because the job is such that it cannot be speeded up, you should assign a MINIMUM of _____ extra men.

    A. 3   B. 4   C. 5   D. 6

13.____

14. Assume that a trench is 42" wide, 5' deep, and 100' long. If the unit price of excavating the trench is $105 per cubic yard, the cost of excavating the trench is MOST NEARLY

    A. $6,805   B. $15,330   C. $21,000   D. $63,000

14.____

15. If the scale on a shop drawing is 1/4 inch to the foot, then the length of a part which measures 2 3/8 inches long on the drawing is ACTUALLY _____ feet.

    A. 9 1/2   B. 8 1/2   C. 7 1/4   D. 4 1/4

15.____

16. It is necessary to pour a new concrete floor for a shop. If the dimensions of the concrete slab for the floor are to be 27' x 18' x 6", then the number of cubic yards of concrete that must be poured is

    A. 9   B. 16   C. 54   D. 243

16.____

17. The jaws of a vise move 1/4" for each complete turn of the handle. The number of complete turns necessary to open the jaws 2 3/4" is

    A. 9   B. 10   C. 11   D. 12

17.____

18. Assume that a jobbing shop is to submit a price for a contract involving 300 pieces of work. Assume that material costs 50 cents per piece, labor costs $7.50 an hour, and a lathe operator can complete 5 pieces in an hour.
If overhead is 40% of material and labor costs and the profit is 10% of all costs, the submitted price for the entire job will be

    A. $630.24   B. $872.80   C. $900.00   D. $924.00

18.____

19. The following formula is used in connection with the three-wire method of measuring   19.____
pitch diameters of screw threads: $G = \dfrac{0.57735}{N}$, where G = wire size and N = number of
threads per inch.
According to this formula, the proper size of wire for a 1"-8NC thread is MOST
NEARLY

    A. .0722"   B. .7217"   C. .0072"   D. .0074"

20. A millimeter is 1/25.4 of an inch and there are 10 millimeters to a centimeter.   20.____
If a piece of stock measures 127 centimeters long, the length of the stock, in feet
and inches, would be MOST NEARLY

    A. 2'1"   B. 4'2"   C. 8'4"   D. 41'8"

21. For a certain job, you will need 25 steel bars 1 inch in diameter and 4"6" long.   21.____
If these bars weigh 3 pounds per foot of length, then the TOTAL weight for all 25 bars is
_____ pounds.

    A. 13.5   B. 75.0   C. 112.5   D. 337.5

22. If steel weighs 0.30 pounds per cubic inch, then the weight of a 2 inch square steel bar   22.____
90 inches long is _____ pounds.

    A. 27   B. 54   C. 108   D. 360

23. A concrete wall is 36' long, 9' high, and 1 1/2' thick. The number of cubic yards of con-   23.____
crete that were needed to make this wall is

    A. 14   B. 18   C. 27   D. 36

24. If the scale on a shop drawing is 1/2 inch to the foot, then the length of a part which mea-   24.____
sures 41/4 inches long on the drawing has a length of APPROXIMATELY _____ feet.

    A. 2 1/8   B. 4 1/4   C. 8 1/2   D. 10 3/4

25. If the allowable load on a wooden scaffold is 60 pounds per square foot and the scaffold   25.____
surface area is 3 feet by 12 feet, then the MAXIMUM total distributed load that is permit-
ted on the scaffold is _____ pounds.

    A. 720   B. 1,800   C. 2,160   D. 2,400

KEY (CORRECT ANSWERS)

1.	A		11.	C
2.	A		12.	D
3.	B		13.	A
4.	D		14.	A
5.	B		15.	A
6.	B		16.	A
7.	C		17.	C
8.	A		18.	D
9.	A		19.	A
10.	B		20.	B

21.	D
22.	C
23.	B
24.	C
25.	C

SOLUTIONS TO PROBLEMS

1. Area = (1/2)(base)(height) = (1/2)(5")(12") = 30 sq.in.

2. Volume = (18") (18") (2") = 648 cu.in. = 648/1720 cu.ft.
   Then, (480)(648/1720) = $\approx$ 180 lbs.

3. 2 cu.yds. = 54 cu.ft. Let x = required cubic feet of sand. Then, 2/5 = x/54. Solving, x = 21.6 (or about 22)

4. (3.75')(25')(4.25') = 398.4375 cu.ft. $\approx$ 14.8 cu.yds.

5. 10'5" + 6'5 1/2" = 16'10 1/2", so lengths of 17 feet are needed

6. The amount of water flowing through each pipe must be equal.

7. (2")(2")(120") = 480 cu. in. Then, (480)(.28) $\approx$ 135 lbs.

8. Volume = (π) (.125 ')^2 (2) $\approx$ .1 cu.ft. Then, (.1)(480) = 48 lbs.

9. (360°)(.05) - 18°

10. 4 1/16 - .006 = 4.0625 - .006 = 4.0565

11. 15 7/16" $\div$ 1/8" = 247/16 . 8/1 = 123.5. Then, (123.5)(1 ft.) = 123.5 ft.

12. 7 3/8" $\div$ 1/4" = 59/8 . 4/1 = 29.5   Then, (29.5)(1 ft.) = 29.5 ft.

13. (6)(4) = 24 man-days normally required. Since after 3 days only the equivalent of (2/3)(24) = 16 man-days of work has been 1 done, 8 man-days of work is still left. 16 $\div$ 3 = 5 1/3, which means the crew is equivalent to only 5 1/3 men. To do the 8 man-days of work, it will require at least 8 - 5 1/3 = 2 2/3 = 3 additional men.

14. (3.5')(5')(100') = 1750 cu.ft. $\approx$ 64.8 cu.yds. Then, (64.8)($105) $\approx$ $6805

15. 2 3/8" $\div$ 1/4" = 19/8 . 4/1 = 9 1/2 Then, (9 1/2)(1 ft.) = 9 1/2 feet

16. (27')(18')(1/2') = 243 cu.ft. = 9 cu.yds. (1 cu.yd. = 27 cu.ft.)

17. 2 3/4" $\div$ 1/4" = 11/4 . 4/1 = 11

18. Material cost = (300)($.50) = $150. Labor cost = ($7.50)(300/5) = $450. Overhead = (.40)($150+$450) = $240. Profit = .10($150+$450+$240) = $84. Submitted price = $150 + $450 + $240 + $84 = $924

19. 6 = .57735" $\div$ 8 = .0722"

20. 127 cm = 1270 mm = 1270/25.4" $\approx$ 50" = 4.2"

21. (25)(4.5') = 112.5' Then, (112.5X3) = 337.5 lbs.

22. (2")(2")(90") = 360 cu.in. Then, (360)(30) = 108 lbs.

23. (36')(9')(1 1/2') = 486 cu.ft. = 18 cu.yds. (1 cu.yd. = 27 cu.ft.)

24. 4 1/4" ÷ 1/2" = 17/4 . 2/1 = 8 1/2. Then, (8 1/2)(1 ft.) = 8 1/2 ft.

25. (12')(3') = 36 sq.ft. Then, (36)(60) = 2160 lbs.

TEST 3

DIRECTIONS: Each question or incomplete statement is followed by several suggested answers or completions. Select the one that BEST answers the question or completes the statement. *PRINT THE LETTER OF THE CORRECT ANSWER IN THE SPACE AT THE RIGHT.*

1. A right triangular metal sheet for a roofing job has sides of 36 inches and 4 feet. The length of the remaining side is

   A. 7 feet   B. 6 feet
   C. 60 inches   D. 90 inches

   1.____

2. A U.S. Standard Gauge thickness is given as 0.15625. This thickness, in fractions of an inch, is MOST NEARLY _____ inches.

   A. 1/8   B. 4/32   C. 5/32   D. 3/64

   2.____

3. The weight per 100 of sheet metal fasteners is given as 2/3 pound. The APPROXIMATE number of fasteners in a 2-pound package is

   A. 166   B. 200   C. 300   D. 266

   3.____

4. The decimal equivalent of 27/32 is MOST NEARLY

   A. 0.813   B. 0.828   C. 0.844   D. 0.859

   4.____

5. If a scaled measurement of 1'3" on the drawing of a sheet metal layout represents an actual length of 10"0", then the drawing has been made to a scale of _____ inch to the foot.

   A. 3/4   B. 1 1/4   C. 1 1/2   D. 1 3/4

   5.____

6. Two and two-thirds tees can be made from one sheet of steel. If 24 tees must be made, then the number of sheets required is

   A. 6   B. 7   C. 8   D. 9

   6.____

7. A main duct 20 inches in diameter discharges into two branch ducts. The sum of the areas of the branches is to be equal to the area of the main duct. One branch is 12 inches in diameter.
   The diameter of the other branch is _____ inches.

   A. 16   B. 12   C. 10   D. 8

   7.____

8. If steel weighs 480 lbs. per cubic foot, the weight of 10 sheets, each 6 feet by 3 feet by 1/32 inch, is _____ lbs.

   A. 2,700   B. 1,237   C. 270   D. 225

   8.____

9. The area, in square inches, of a right triangle that has sides of 12 1/2, 10, and 7 1/2 inches is

   A. 18 1/4   B. 37 1/2   C. 75   D. 60

   9.____

10. In making a container to hold 1 gallon (231 cu.in.) and to be 6 inches in diameter at the top and 8 inches in diameter at the bottom, the height must be, in inches,

  A. 10.0   B. 8.2   C. 4.6   D. 6   10.____

11. A sheet metal worker is given a job to make a transition piece from a 8 1/2" diameter duct to an 11 1/4" diameter duct. If the length of the transition piece is 5 1/2" for each inch change in diameter, then the length of the transition piece is

  A. 14 7/8"   B. 15"   C. 15 1/8"   D. 15 1/4"   11.____

12. A duct layout is drawn to a scale of 3/8" to a foot. If the length of a run shown on the drawing scales 7 1/2", then the ACTUAL length of the run is

  A. 19'6"   B. 19'9"   C. 20'0"   D. 20'3"   12.____

13. An 18" x 24" duct is to be connected to a 24" x 24" duct by means of an eccentric transition piece (3 sides flush). If the taper is to be 1" in 4", then the length of the transition piece is

  A. 6"   B. 12"   C. 18"   D. 24"   13.____

14. Twenty-seven pairs of 3/8" diameter rods each 3'3 1/2" long are needed to support a duct.
If the available rods are ten feet long, then the MINIMUM number of rods that will be needed to make the twenty-seven sets is

  A. 9   B. 12   C. 15   D. 18   14.____

15. A rectangular sheet metal air duct with open ends is 12 feet long and 15" x 20" in cross-section. If one square foot of the sheet metal weighs 1/2 pound, then the TOTAL weight of the duct is _____ lbs.

  A. 10   B. 17 1/2   C. 35   D. 150   15.____

16. The sum of 1/12 and 1/4 is

  A. 1/3   B. 5/12   C. 7/12   D. 3/8   16.____

17. The product of 12 and 2 1/3 is

  A. 27   B. 28   C. 29   D. 30   17.____

18. If 4 1/2 is subtracted from 7 1/5, the remainder is

  A. 3 7/10   B. 2 7/10   C. 3 3/10   D. 2 3/10   18.____

19. The number of cubic yards in 47 cubic feet is MOST NEARLY

  A. 1.70   B. 1.74   C. 1.78   D. 1.82   19.____

20. A wall 8'0" high by 12'6" long has a window opening 4'0" high by 3'6" wide. The net area of the wall (allowing for the window opening) is, in square feet,

  A. 86   B. 87   C. 88   D. 89   20.____

21. A worker's hourly rate is $11.36.
    If he works 11 1/2 hours, he should receive

    A. $129.84   B. $130.64   C. $131.48   D. $132.24

22. The number of cubic feet in 3 cubic yards is

    A. 81   B. 82   C. 83   D. 84

23. At an annual rate of $.40 per $100, what is the fire insurance premium for one year on a house that is insured for $80,000?

    A. $120   B. $160   C. $240   D. $320

24. A meter equals approximately 1.09 yards.
    How much longer, in yards, is a 100-meter dash than a 100-yard dash?

    A. 6   B. 8   C. 9   D. 12

25. A train leaves New York City at 8:10 A.M. and arrives in Buffalo at 4:45 P.M. on the same day. How long, in hours and minutes, does it take the train to make the trip?
    _____ hours, _____ minutes.

    A. 6; 22   B. 7; 16   C. 7; 28   D. 8; 35

21._____
22._____
23._____
24._____
25._____

KEY (CORRECT ANSWERS)

1.	C	11.	C
2.	C	12.	C
3.	C	13.	D
4.	C	14.	D
5.	C	15.	C
6.	D	16.	A
7.	A	17.	B
8.	D	18.	B
9.	B	19.	B
10.	D	20.	A

21. B
22. A
23. D
24. C
25. D

SOLUTIONS TO PROBLEMS

1. Let x = remaining side. Converting to inches, $x^2 = 36^2 + 48^2$ So, $x^2 = 3600$. Solving, x = 60 inches.

2. $.15625 = \dfrac{15,625}{100,000} = \dfrac{5}{32}$

3. $2 \div 2/3 = 3$. Then, (3)(100) = 300 fasteners

4. $27/32 = .84375 \approx .844$

5. 1'3" ÷ 10 = 15" ÷ 10 = 1 1/2"

6. 24 ÷ 2 2/3 = 24/1.3/8 = 9

7. Area of main duct = $(\pi)(10^2) = 100\pi$. One of the branches has an area of $(\pi)(6^2) = 36\pi$. Thus, the area of the 2nd branch = $100\pi - 36\pi = 64\pi$. The 2nd branch's radius must be 8" and its diameter must be 16".

8. Volume = (1/384')(6')(3') = .046875 cu.ft. Then, 10 sheets have a volume of .46875 cu.ft. Now, (.46875)(480) = 225 lbs.

9. Note that $(7\,1/2)^2 + (10)^2 = (12\,1/2)^2$, so that this is a right triangle. Area = (1/2)(10")(7 1/2") = 37 1/2 sq.in.

10. $231 = \dfrac{h}{3}[(\pi)(3)^2 + (\pi)(4)^2 + \sqrt{(9\pi)(16\pi)]},$ where h = required height. Then,

    $231 = \dfrac{h}{3}(9\pi + 16\pi + 12\pi).$ Simplifying, $231 = 37\pi h/3$.
    Solving, h ~ 5.96" or 6"

11. 11 1/4 - 8 1/2 = 2 3/4. Then, (2 3/4)(5 1/2) = 11/4 . 11/2 = 15 1/8

12. 7 1/2 " ÷ 3/8" = 15/2 . 8/3 = 20 Then, (20)(1 ft.) = 20 feet

13. 24" - 18" = 6" Then, (6")(4) = 24"

14. 3'3 1/2" = 39.5". Now, (27)(2)(39.5") = 2133". 10 ft. = 120".
    Finally, 2133 ÷ 120 = 17.775, so 18 rods are needed.

15. Surface area = (2)(12')(1 1/4') + (2)(12')(1 2/3') = 70 sq.ft.
    Then, (70)(1/2 lb.) - 35 lbs.

16. 1/12 + 1/4 = 4/12 = 1/3

17. $(12)(2\ 1/3) = 12/1 \cdot 7/3 = 28$

18. $7\ 1/5 - 4\ 1/2 = 7\ 2/10 - 4\ 5/10 = 6\ 12/10 - 4\ 5/10 = 2\ 7/10$

19.   47 cu.ft. = 47/27 cu.yds. = 1.74 cu.yds.

20. $(8')(12.5') - (4')(3.5') = 86$ sq.ft.

21. $(\$11.36)(11.5) = \$130.64$

22.   1 cu.yd. = 27 cu.ft., so 3 cu.yds. = 81 cu.ft.

23. $\$80,000 \div \$100 = 800$. Then, $(800)(\$.40) = \$320$

24.   100 meters = 109 yds. Then, 109 - 100 = 9 yds.

25.   4:45 P.M. - 8:10 AM. = 8 hrs. 35 min.

ANSWER SHEET

TEST NO. _____ PART _____ TITLE OF POSITION _____
                                                    (AS GIVEN IN EXAMINATION ANNOUNCEMENT - INCLUDE OPTION, IF ANY)

PLACE OF EXAMINATION _____ DATE _____

| | (CITY OR TOWN) | (STATE) | | RATING |

USE THE SPECIAL PENCIL.   MAKE GLOSSY BLACK MARKS.

	A B C D E		A B C D E		A B C D E		A B C D E		A B C D E
1		26		51		76		101	
2		27		52		77		102	
3		28		53		78		103	
4		29		54		79		104	
5		30		55		80		105	
6		31		56		81		106	
7		32		57		82		107	
8		33		58		83		108	
9		34		59		84		109	
10		35		60		85		110	

Make only ONE mark for each answer.   Additional and stray marks may be
counted as mistakes.   In making corrections, erase errors COMPLETELY.

	A B C D E		A B C D E		A B C D E		A B C D E		A B C D E
11		36		61		86		111	
12		37		62		87		112	
13		38		63		88		113	
14		39		64		89		114	
15		40		65		90		115	
16		41		66		91		116	
17		42		67		92		117	
18		43		68		93		118	
19		44		69		94		119	
20		45		70		95		120	
21		46		71		96		121	
22		47		72		97		122	
23		48		73		98		123	
24		49		74		99		124	
25		50		75		100		125	

ANSWER SHEET

TEST NO. _____ PART _____ TITLE OF POSITION _____

(AS GIVEN IN EXAMINATION ANNOUNCEMENT - INCLUDE OPTION, IF ANY)

PLACE OF EXAMINATION _____ DATE _____

(CITY OR TOWN)   (STATE)

RATING

USE THE SPECIAL PENCIL.   MAKE GLOSSY BLACK MARKS.

	A B C D E		A B C D E		A B C D E		A B C D E		A B C D E
1	⋮ ⋮ ⋮ ⋮ ⋮	26	⋮ ⋮ ⋮ ⋮ ⋮	51	⋮ ⋮ ⋮ ⋮ ⋮	76	⋮ ⋮ ⋮ ⋮ ⋮	101	⋮ ⋮ ⋮ ⋮ ⋮
2	⋮ ⋮ ⋮ ⋮ ⋮	27	⋮ ⋮ ⋮ ⋮ ⋮	52	⋮ ⋮ ⋮ ⋮ ⋮	77	⋮ ⋮ ⋮ ⋮ ⋮	102	⋮ ⋮ ⋮ ⋮ ⋮
3	⋮ ⋮ ⋮ ⋮ ⋮	28	⋮ ⋮ ⋮ ⋮ ⋮	53	⋮ ⋮ ⋮ ⋮ ⋮	78	⋮ ⋮ ⋮ ⋮ ⋮	103	⋮ ⋮ ⋮ ⋮ ⋮
4	⋮ ⋮ ⋮ ⋮ ⋮	29	⋮ ⋮ ⋮ ⋮ ⋮	54	⋮ ⋮ ⋮ ⋮ ⋮	79	⋮ ⋮ ⋮ ⋮ ⋮	104	⋮ ⋮ ⋮ ⋮ ⋮
5	⋮ ⋮ ⋮ ⋮ ⋮	30	⋮ ⋮ ⋮ ⋮ ⋮	55	⋮ ⋮ ⋮ ⋮ ⋮	80	⋮ ⋮ ⋮ ⋮ ⋮	105	⋮ ⋮ ⋮ ⋮ ⋮
6	⋮ ⋮ ⋮ ⋮ ⋮	31	⋮ ⋮ ⋮ ⋮ ⋮	56	⋮ ⋮ ⋮ ⋮ ⋮	81	⋮ ⋮ ⋮ ⋮ ⋮	106	⋮ ⋮ ⋮ ⋮ ⋮
7	⋮ ⋮ ⋮ ⋮ ⋮	32	⋮ ⋮ ⋮ ⋮ ⋮	57	⋮ ⋮ ⋮ ⋮ ⋮	82	⋮ ⋮ ⋮ ⋮ ⋮	107	⋮ ⋮ ⋮ ⋮ ⋮
8	⋮ ⋮ ⋮ ⋮ ⋮	33	⋮ ⋮ ⋮ ⋮ ⋮	58	⋮ ⋮ ⋮ ⋮ ⋮	83	⋮ ⋮ ⋮ ⋮ ⋮	108	⋮ ⋮ ⋮ ⋮ ⋮
9	⋮ ⋮ ⋮ ⋮ ⋮	34	⋮ ⋮ ⋮ ⋮ ⋮	59	⋮ ⋮ ⋮ ⋮ ⋮	84	⋮ ⋮ ⋮ ⋮ ⋮	109	⋮ ⋮ ⋮ ⋮ ⋮
10	⋮ ⋮ ⋮ ⋮ ⋮	35	⋮ ⋮ ⋮ ⋮ ⋮	60	⋮ ⋮ ⋮ ⋮ ⋮	85	⋮ ⋮ ⋮ ⋮ ⋮	110	⋮ ⋮ ⋮ ⋮ ⋮

Make only ONE mark for each answer.   Additional and stray marks may be
counted as mistakes.   In making corrections, erase errors COMPLETELY.

	A B C D E		A B C D E		A B C D E		A B C D E		A B C D E
11	⋮ ⋮ ⋮ ⋮ ⋮	36	⋮ ⋮ ⋮ ⋮ ⋮	61	⋮ ⋮ ⋮ ⋮ ⋮	86	⋮ ⋮ ⋮ ⋮ ⋮	111	⋮ ⋮ ⋮ ⋮ ⋮
12	⋮ ⋮ ⋮ ⋮ ⋮	37	⋮ ⋮ ⋮ ⋮ ⋮	62	⋮ ⋮ ⋮ ⋮ ⋮	87	⋮ ⋮ ⋮ ⋮ ⋮	112	⋮ ⋮ ⋮ ⋮ ⋮
13	⋮ ⋮ ⋮ ⋮ ⋮	38	⋮ ⋮ ⋮ ⋮ ⋮	63	⋮ ⋮ ⋮ ⋮ ⋮	88	⋮ ⋮ ⋮ ⋮ ⋮	113	⋮ ⋮ ⋮ ⋮ ⋮
14	⋮ ⋮ ⋮ ⋮ ⋮	39	⋮ ⋮ ⋮ ⋮ ⋮	64	⋮ ⋮ ⋮ ⋮ ⋮	89	⋮ ⋮ ⋮ ⋮ ⋮	114	⋮ ⋮ ⋮ ⋮ ⋮
15	⋮ ⋮ ⋮ ⋮ ⋮	40	⋮ ⋮ ⋮ ⋮ ⋮	65	⋮ ⋮ ⋮ ⋮ ⋮	90	⋮ ⋮ ⋮ ⋮ ⋮	115	⋮ ⋮ ⋮ ⋮ ⋮
16	⋮ ⋮ ⋮ ⋮ ⋮	41	⋮ ⋮ ⋮ ⋮ ⋮	66	⋮ ⋮ ⋮ ⋮ ⋮	91	⋮ ⋮ ⋮ ⋮ ⋮	116	⋮ ⋮ ⋮ ⋮ ⋮
17	⋮ ⋮ ⋮ ⋮ ⋮	42	⋮ ⋮ ⋮ ⋮ ⋮	67	⋮ ⋮ ⋮ ⋮ ⋮	92	⋮ ⋮ ⋮ ⋮ ⋮	117	⋮ ⋮ ⋮ ⋮ ⋮
18	⋮ ⋮ ⋮ ⋮ ⋮	43	⋮ ⋮ ⋮ ⋮ ⋮	68	⋮ ⋮ ⋮ ⋮ ⋮	93	⋮ ⋮ ⋮ ⋮ ⋮	118	⋮ ⋮ ⋮ ⋮ ⋮
19	⋮ ⋮ ⋮ ⋮ ⋮	44	⋮ ⋮ ⋮ ⋮ ⋮	69	⋮ ⋮ ⋮ ⋮ ⋮	94	⋮ ⋮ ⋮ ⋮ ⋮	119	⋮ ⋮ ⋮ ⋮ ⋮
20	⋮ ⋮ ⋮ ⋮ ⋮	45	⋮ ⋮ ⋮ ⋮ ⋮	70	⋮ ⋮ ⋮ ⋮ ⋮	95	⋮ ⋮ ⋮ ⋮ ⋮	120	⋮ ⋮ ⋮ ⋮ ⋮
21	⋮ ⋮ ⋮ ⋮ ⋮	46	⋮ ⋮ ⋮ ⋮ ⋮	71	⋮ ⋮ ⋮ ⋮ ⋮	96	⋮ ⋮ ⋮ ⋮ ⋮	121	⋮ ⋮ ⋮ ⋮ ⋮
22	⋮ ⋮ ⋮ ⋮ ⋮	47	⋮ ⋮ ⋮ ⋮ ⋮	72	⋮ ⋮ ⋮ ⋮ ⋮	97	⋮ ⋮ ⋮ ⋮ ⋮	122	⋮ ⋮ ⋮ ⋮ ⋮
23	⋮ ⋮ ⋮ ⋮ ⋮	48	⋮ ⋮ ⋮ ⋮ ⋮	73	⋮ ⋮ ⋮ ⋮ ⋮	98	⋮ ⋮ ⋮ ⋮ ⋮	123	⋮ ⋮ ⋮ ⋮ ⋮
24	⋮ ⋮ ⋮ ⋮ ⋮	49	⋮ ⋮ ⋮ ⋮ ⋮	74	⋮ ⋮ ⋮ ⋮ ⋮	99	⋮ ⋮ ⋮ ⋮ ⋮	124	⋮ ⋮ ⋮ ⋮ ⋮
25	⋮ ⋮ ⋮ ⋮ ⋮	50	⋮ ⋮ ⋮ ⋮ ⋮	75	⋮ ⋮ ⋮ ⋮ ⋮	100	⋮ ⋮ ⋮ ⋮ ⋮	125	⋮ ⋮ ⋮ ⋮ ⋮